Hands-On Word Family Activities for Young Readers

Ready-to-Use Lessons and Activities for Building Literacy Skills

Roberta Seckler Brown

Susan Carey

JOSSEY-BASS
A Wiley Imprint
www.josseybass.com

Published by Jossey-Bass
A Wiley Imprint
989 Market Street, San Francisco, CA 94103-1741   www.josseybass.com

Jossey-Bass books and products are available through most bookstores. To contact Jossey-Bass directly, call our Customer Care Department within the U.S. at (800) 956-7739, outside the U.S. at (317) 572-3993 or fax (317) 572-4002.

Jossey-Bass also publishes its books in a variety of electronic formats. Some content that appears in print may not be available in electronic books.

Library of Congress Cataloging-in-Publication Data

Brown, Roberta Seckler.
    Hands-on word family activities for young readers : ready-to-use
lessons and activities for building literacy skills / Roberta Seckler
Brown, Susan Carey.
        p. cm.
Includes bibliographical references.
    ISBN 0-7879-6592-8 (pbk. : alk. paper)
    1. Reading (Kindergarten) 2. Reading (Primary) 3. Word recognition.
4. Reading—Phonetic method. I. Carey, Susan. II. Title.
    LB1181.4.B76 2003
    372.4—dc21

                                                        2002155632

Printed in the United States of America

FIRST EDITION

PB Printing 10 9 8 7 6 5 4 3 2 1

About the Authors

ROBERTA SECKLER BROWN received her B.A. from Fordham University and her master's degree as a reading specialist from St. John's University. Mrs. Brown is also certified by New York University as a Reading Recovery teacher.

SUSAN CAREY received her B.S. from the State University College of New York at Brockport and her master's degree in early childhood education from Western Connecticut University. Mrs. Carey is also certified by New York University as a Reading Recovery teacher.

The authors have previously published *Hands-On Alphabet Activities for Young Children: A Whole Language Plus Phonics Approach to Reading* (The Center for Applied Research in Education, 1998), and *Hide and Seek* and *The Tree House* (Scholastic Inc., 1994).

Sue and Roberta have taught kindergarten and are currently teaching a collaborative first grade at the Park Early Childhood Center for the Ossining Public Schools in New York.

About This Book

Hands-On Word Family Activities for Young Readers is a comprehensive and thorough literacy study book that presents children with real reading experiences by teaching word families in context. This approach allows children the opportunity to learn and practice the essential phonological skills of onset and rime while they are reading an engaging yet challenging story or poem. Primary, Reading, Resource Room, English as a Second Language, and Special Education teachers can use this book for whole group, small group, or individual instruction.

This unique resource uses poems, big books, individual take-home (little) books, word family concept cans, word family blending strips, art activities, and flashcards to reinforce the particular word family being taught. From the very first day, the children are *reading* poems and books that have been specifically written to teach a word family.

Included in the easy-to-follow lessons for each word family are:

- an objective for the day
- materials needed
- an introduction
- specific procedures
- art activity
- independent activity
- challenge activity
- reinforcement activity
- reproducible line masters
- related pocket chart interactions

By actively involving students in real reading experiences, *Hands-On Word Family Activities for Young Readers* builds self-esteem and increases independence as students learn to master the word families.

Reading—Through hands-on reading, children practice all of the essential book-handling skills and reading strategies necessary to become a fluent and independent reader.

Word Family Study—Each poem and book is based on one word family, focusing the children on the "chunk" or part of a word they know. Children will learn how to use this knowledge as a strategy to help them read unfamiliar words with the same chunk.

Self-Esteem—Children are challenged by putting together all of the isolated skills they are learning. The rewards are successful reading and increased confidence as they begin to see themselves as independent readers.

Independence—As children become independent readers, they begin to take ownership of their learning. The take-home books are designed to be consumable. Children may color in the illustrations and it becomes their book.

The word families in this book are presented in alphabetical order for reference purposes only. Sections can be selected and used as needed to supplement your literacy curriculum.

We have successfully used all of the components of this book with our own students. We wish you and your students the same success we have experienced!

Roberta Seckler Brown and Susan Carey

How to Use This Book

Hands-On Word Family Activities for Young Readers is divided into 25 sections, one for each word family. Each section contains three daily lesson plans. The structure of the lesson plans is consistent throughout the book.

- **Lesson 1**—In the first lesson, children learn to visually recognize the designated word family anchor word. The anchor word is introduced in a short poem, which can be displayed in a big chart-sized format. A follow-up art activity that reinforces the anchor word is also included in this lesson. Line masters are provided for the art activity and poem.

- **Lesson 2**—Children will recognize the word family "chunk" visually and auditorily, and read words in that word family. The word family words are introduced in a longer poem. The children are taught to recognize the chunk and notice how the initial letter/letters can be changed to create many words within the same word family.

   Children will also make their own word family blending strip and use it to form words that they will read to you. They may take home the blending strip and read the words again.

   Flashcard line masters for the word family being studied are included in this lesson. You may use these in class or send them home with the students.

   Challenge and reinforcement activities are provided in this lesson so you can differentiate instruction according to the individual needs of your students.

- **Lesson 3**—Children will read a Big Book and a Little Book to integrate the specific word family strategies they have learned. You will read the Big Book together and label the pictures in the word family under study. Then children will read the Little Book independently or with a partner. You may wish to have the children take the book home and read it to an adult.

   As an additional activity, you may choose to have the children create sentences using words from the word family being studied. This will provide extra practice in reading the words in context.

Included in "How to Use This Book" are instructions for making the materials for teaching the lessons. (See page viii.) You will need to make these materials prior to teaching each word family.

1. Word family concept cans
2. Chart-sized poems

3. Little Books
4. Big Books
5. Blending strips
6. Flashcards

Each section includes line masters for take-home (little) books, big books, poems, art activities, and flashcards.

Hands-On Word Family Activities for Young Readers gives specific step-by-step instructions for teaching word families in isolation and in context. Each word family study is presented in the same sequence. This makes the book teacher-friendly and provides students with continuity of instruction. As teachers, we know how important continuity is for all students. When children can anticipate what is next, it alleviates anxiety and empowers them as learners.

The following books are recommended for reading aloud with children in several of the lessons to activate prior knowledge and to introduce the word families under study.

A Bad Case of Stripes by David Shannon. Blue Sky Press, 1998

Andrew's Loose Tooth by Robert Munsch. Scholastic, 1998

Chicken Soup With Rice by Maurice Sendak. Harper Trophy, 1991

Froggy Gets Dressed by Jonathan London. Scholastic, 1995

Gilberto and the Wind by Marie Hall Ets. Viking Press, 1963

Go, Dog, Go! by P. D. Eastman. Random House, 1961

Harry the Dirty Dog by Gene Zion. Harper & Row Publishers, 1956

Mop Top by Don Freeman. Puffin Books, 1978

Snow by Roy McKie and P. D. Eastman. Random House, 1962

The Best Nest by P. D. Eastman. Random House, 1968

The Cake That Mack Ate by Rose Robart. Atlantic Monthly Press, 1987

The Snowy Day by Ezra Jack Keats. Viking, 1963

The Tortoise and the Hare, an Aesop fable adapted by Janet Stevens. Holiday House, 1984

We Are All Alike . . . We Are All Different, written and illustrated by Cheltenham Elementary Kindergartners. Scholastic, 1991

Winter (Get Set . . . Go) by Ruth Thomson. Children's Press, 1994

Instructions for Making . . .

1. WORD FAMILY CONCEPT CANS

Materials:
- 25 small clear plastic tubs (with lids)
- Black permanent marker

Directions:

1. Write the "chunk" of the word family on the lid of the tub.

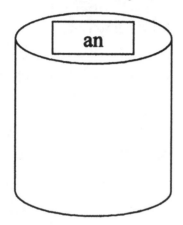

2. Fill the tub with items appropriate for the word family that appears on the top of the tub.
3. Repeat this procedure for each of the 25 word families.

Note: The concept cans are intended to fill in the gaps for those students who may have limited or no prior knowledge of the word-family words. You may not be able to find an item for each word in the word family. You may substitute a picture of the word if an item is not possible.

2. CHART-SIZED POEMS

Materials:
- One 24" × 36" piece of lined chart paper for each poem you are making
- Black permanent marker

Directions:

1. Using the word family poem in the first lesson for each word family as a guide, write the poem as it appears.

2. Make sure to leave enough space between the lines so the poem does not appear visually confusing.
3. Laminate if possible.
4. Repeat steps 1–3 using the word family poem in the second lesson. You will actually be making two chart-sized poems for each word family.

3. LITTLE BOOKS

Materials:

- Line masters of the word family book you are making
- Stapler
- Paper cutter

Directions:

1. Reproduce one complete copy of the Little Book you are making for each child.
2. Cut the pages in half horizontally, so they are even.
3. Collate pages, making sure they are in the correct order.
4. Staple along the left side of the book.

4. BIG BOOKS

Materials:

- Seven 12" × 18" white pieces of construction paper for each book you are making
- One 12" × 18" piece of colored construction paper for each book you are making
- Permanent black marker
- Stapler
- Line master of Big Book pictures for the word-family book you are making
- Crayons or water-based markers for coloring in line masters
- Scissors

Directions:

1. Photocopy line masters of Big Book pictures for the word family book you are making.
2. Cut out and color the pictures.
3. Place the white paper horizontally. Glue one picture on each page, 3 inches from the top and centered.

4. Make sure to leave a 3-inch margin from the left when you begin writing the words.
5. Using the Little Book as a guide, write the text under each picture.
6. Then write the title on the piece of colored construction paper.
7. Staple along the left side of the book.

5. BLENDING STRIPS

Materials:
- Line master for blending strip you are making
- Scissors
- Paper cutter
- One 11" × 1" piece of tagboard (natural or white only) per child
- Permanent black marker

Directions:
1. Reproduce one blending strip line master per child.
2. Cut one 11" × 1" piece of tagboard per child.
3. Carefully print the letters for the blending strip on each piece of tagboard. Make sure to leave a finger space between each letter. You will find the designated letters for each strip in Lesson 2 of each word family.
4. Make one extra blending strip to use as the model for the blending strip activity found in Lesson 2 of each word family.
5. Cut two 1-inch vertical slits to the left of the chunk printed on the blending strip. Be sure to leave a 1-inch space between the slits.
6. Slide the strip through the slits. Here is an example.

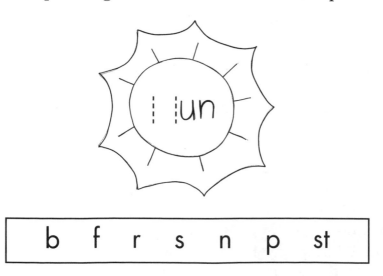

6. FLASHCARDS

Materials:

- Line master of flashcards for the word family you are studying
- Scissors or paper cutter

Directions:

1. Reproduce one line master of flashcards per child.
2. Cut the flashcards on the lines provided.

Related Pocket Chart Interactions

Pocket charts are a valuable teaching tool. They can be used either in whole class, small group, or individual learning center situations. The following are some ways to integrate pocket charts into your word family instruction. You may use these suggestions in the following ways: at the beginning of your word family study to gather information about how much your students already know about a particular word family, during word family instruction to reinforce the word family chunk being taught, as a follow-up activity, or for individual practice in a learning center.

Directions:

Holding a 5" × 8" index card horizontally, print a letter card for each letter of the alphabet. You will need to make several sets as you will use them for word family instruction. *Note:* Some teachers like to print the multiple letter word family "chunk" being studied together on an index card rather than use the individual letter cards.

Procedure:

1. Hold up the card or cards for the word family being presented.
2. Tell children the name of the letters and then say the sound of the "chunk"; for example, *a, n, an.*
3. Have the children repeat: *a, n, an.*
4. Place the letters in the pocket chart.
5. Have children read the chunk.
6. Place a letter in front of the chunk to create a new word: *c, an.*
7. Show the children how to blend the new letter with the chunk.
8. Repeat this procedure with as many of the consonants as you like.
9. To differentiate instruction, include various consonant blends and digraphs.

The pocket chart may be left in a language center for the children so they can actively interact with and manipulate the letters to create new words. Paper and pencil should be available for those students who wish to copy the word-family words. The kinesthetic act of writing helps the children internalize the material they are learning.

Word Family Concept Cans

Current educational research states that children need a solid language base and a basic vocabulary before they can read. As teachers, we know that many of our students come to us lacking a well-developed vocabulary and understanding of many basic language concepts. Concept cans are a valuable tool for filling in the gaps for these children and for activating prior knowledge of other children. Below are just a few suggestions about how to use the concept cans. You may integrate concept cans into your word family study however you feel appropriate. Concept cans can be integrated in a variety of ways: at the beginning of your word family study to gather information about how much your students already know about a particular word family, during word family instruction to reinforce the word family "chunk" being taught, as a follow-up activity, or for individual practice in a learning center.

Directions:
- Choose the word family to be studied.
- Make sure the concept can has as many items and/or pictures in it as you can find for that word family. The more the better!

Procedure:
1. Tell the children the "chunk" you are studying; for example, *an.*
2. Tell children that you have a tub or can that contains things that are part of the ____ word family. Ask the children to predict what they might find in the concept can for that word family.
3. You may record their predictions so they visually see the chunk being studied or you may use this as an oral language activity.
4. When the students are finished predicting, (very dramatically) pull each item from the concept can one at a time. **Make sure you label each item for the children.** You do not want them to hear the wrong word and have that word become part of their memory for the chunk. Have each child repeat the name of the item after you. Make sure students know what each item is. This is the whole point of the concept cans, to fill in gaps for those with little or no prior experiences.
5. If you have written the predictions, make sure you review them with the children so there is closure for that activity.
6. If you have not previously written down the students' predictions, you may want to now write a list of the items found in the can, thus providing a phonetic component to the phonological activity.

Contents

About This Book   iv

How to Use This Book   vi

Instructions for Making . . .

    Word Family Concept Cans   viii

    Chart-Sized Poems   viii

    Little Books   ix

    Big Books   ix

    Blending Strips   x

    Flashcards   xi

Related Pocket Chart Interactions   xii

Word Family Concept Cans   xiii

Word Family: -ake   1

Lesson 1: Objectives (1), Materials (1), Procedure (1), "My Big Cake" Poem (1), Art Activity (2), Conclusion of Lesson (2), Line Master—"My Big Cake" Poem (3), Line Master—Cake (4)

Lesson 2: Objectives (5), Materials (5), Procedure (5), "Jake the Snake" Poem (5), -ake Blending Strip Activity (6), Challenge Activity (7), Reinforcement Activity (7), Line Master—Snake (8), Flashcards (9)

Lesson 3: Objective (10), Materials (10), Procedure (10), Line Masters—Little Book (11), Line Masters—Big Book (15)

Word Family: -am   22

Lesson 1: Objectives (22), Materials (22), Procedure (22), "I Am!" Poem (22), Art Activity (23), Conclusion of Lesson (23), Line Master—"I Am!" Poem (24), Line Master—"I Am!" Border (25)

Lesson 2: Objectives (26), Materials (26), Procedure (26), "Picnic at the Dam" Poem (26), -am Blending Strip Activity (27), Challenge Activity (28), Reinforcement Activity (28), Line Master—Jam Jar (29), Flashcards (30)

Lesson 3: Objective (31), Materials (31), Procedure (31), Line Masters—Little Book (32), Line Masters—Big Book (36)

Word Family: -ame 43

Lesson 1: Objectives (43), Materials (43), Procedure (43), "Games" Poem (43), Art Activity (44), Conclusion of Lesson (44), Line Master—"Games" Poem (45), Line Master—Board Game (46)

Lesson 2: Objectives (47), Materials (47), Procedure (47), "The Word Game" Poem (47), -ame Blending Strip Activity (48), Challenge Activity (49), Reinforcement Activity (49), Line Master—Frame (50), Flashcards (51)

Lesson 3: Objective (52), Materials (52), Procedure (52), Line Masters—Little Book (53), Line Masters—Big Book (57)

Word Family: -an 64

Lesson 1: Objectives (64), Materials (64), Procedure (64), "I Can!" Poem (64), Art Activity (65), Conclusion of Lesson (65), Line Master—"I Can!" Poem (66), Line Master—"I Can!" Border (67)

Lesson 2: Objectives (68), Materials (68), Procedure (68), "Stan and Jan" Poem (68), -an Blending Strip Activity (69), Challenge Activity (70), Reinforcement Activity (70), Line Master—Can (71), Flashcards (72)

Lesson 3: Objective (73), Materials (73), Procedure (73), Line Masters—Little Book (74), Line Masters—Big Book (78)

Word Family: -at 85

Lesson 1: Objectives (85), Materials (85), Procedure (85), "Cats, Cats, Cats" Poem (85), Art Activity (86), Conclusion of Lesson (86), Line Master—"Cats, Cats, Cats" Poem (87), Line Master—Cat (88)

Lesson 2:   Objectives (89), Materials (89), Procedure (89),
            "Pat the Fat Cat" Poem (89), -at Blending
            Strip Activity (90), Challenge Activity (91),
            Reinforcement Activity (91), Line Master—Hat
            (92), Flashcards (93)

Lesson 3:   Objective (94), Materials (94), Procedure (94),
            Line Masters—Little Book (95), Line
            Masters—Big Book (99)

Word Family: -ay   106

Lesson 1:   Objectives (106), Materials (106), Procedure
            (106), "What Kind of Day?" Poem (106), Art
            Activity (107), Conclusion of Lesson (107),
            Line Master—"What Kind of Day?" Poem
            (108), Line Master—Weather Picture (109)

Lesson 2:   Objectives (110), Materials (110), Procedure
            (110), "Play All Day" Poem (110), -ay Blending
            Strip Activity (111), Challenge Activity (112),
            Reinforcement Activity (112), Line Master—
            Hay (113), Flashcards (114)

Lesson 3:   Objective (115), Materials (115), Procedure
            (115), Line Masters—Little Book (116), Line
            Masters—Big Book (120)

Word Family: -ed   127

Lesson 1:   Objectives (127), Materials (127), Procedure
            (127), "My Cozy Bed" Poem (127), Art Activity
            (128), Conclusion of Lesson (128), Line
            Master—"My Cozy Bed" Poem (129), Line
            Master—Bed (130)

Lesson 2:   Objectives (131), Materials (131), Procedure
            (131), "My Red Sled" Poem (131), -ed
            Blending Strip Activity (132), Challenge
            Activity (133), Reinforcement Activity (133),
            Line Master—Red Crayon (134), Flashcards
            (135)

Lesson 3:   Objective (136), Materials (136), Procedure
            (136), Line Masters—Little Book (137), Line
            Masters—Big Book (141)

Word Family: -ell 148

Lesson 1: Objectives (148), Materials (148), Procedure (148), "The Wishing Well" Poem (148), Art Activity (149), Conclusion of Lesson (149), Line Master—"The Wishing Well" Poem (150), Line Master—Wishing Well (151)

Lesson 2: Objectives (152), Materials (152), Procedure (152), "Show and Tell" Poem (152), -cll Blending Strip Activity (153), Challenge Activity (154), Reinforcement Activity (154), Line Master—Bell (155), Flashcards (156)

Lesson 3: Objective (157), Materials (157), Procedure (157), Line Masters—Little Book (158), Line Masters—Big Book (162)

Word Family: -est 169

Lesson 1: Objectives (169), Materials (169), Procedure (169), "My Little Nest" Poem (169), Art Activity (170), Conclusion of Lesson (170), Line Master—"My Little Nest" Poem (171), Line Master—Bird (172)

Lesson 2: Objectives (173), Materials (173), Procedure (173), "The Wild West" Poem (173), -est Blending Strip Activity (174), Challenge Activity (175), Reinforcement Activity (175), Line Master—Vest (176), Flashcards (177)

Lesson 3: Objective (178), Materials (178), Procedure (178), Line Masters—Little Book (179), Line Masters—Big Book (183)

Word Family: -et 190

Lesson 1: Objectives (190), Materials (190), Procedure (190), "Get Set!" Poem (190), Art Activity (191), Conclusion of Lesson (191), Line Master—"Get Set!" Poem (192), Line Master—Person (193)

Lesson 2: Objectives (194), Materials (194), Procedure (194), "The Birthday Pet" Poem (194), -et Blending Strip Activity (195), Challenge Activity (196), Reinforcement Activity (196), Line Master—Jet (197), Flashcards (198)

Lesson 3: Objective (199), Materials (199), Procedure
           (199), Line Masters—Little Book (200), Line
           Masters—Big Book (204)

Word Family: -ice   211

Lesson 1: Objectives (211), Materials (211), Procedure
           (211), "Roll the Dice" Poem (211), Art Activity
           (212), Conclusion of Lesson (212), Line
           Master—"Roll the Dice" Poem (213), Line
           Master—Die (214)

Lesson 2: Objectives (215), Materials (215), Procedure
           (215), "Twice-Cooked Rice" Poem (215), -ice
           Blending Strip Activity (216), Challenge
           Activity (217), Reinforcement Activity (217),
           Line Master—Mice (218), Flashcards (219)

Lesson 3: Objective (220), Materials (220), Procedure
           (220), Line Masters—Little Book (221), Line
           Masters—Big Book (225)

Word Family: -ide   232

Lesson 1: Objectives (232), Materials (232), Procedure
           (232), "Ride Up and Away!" Poem (232), Art
           Activity (233), Conclusion of Lesson (233),
           Line Master—"Ride Up and Away!" Poem
           (234), Line Master—Hot Air Balloon (235)

Lesson 2: Objectives (236), Materials (236), Procedure
           (236), "Let's Ride" Poem (236), -ide Blending
           Strip Activity (237), Challenge Activity (238),
           Reinforcement Activity (238), Line Master—
           Slide (239), Flashcards (240)

Lesson 3: Objective (241), Materials (241), Procedure
           (241), Line Masters—Little Book (242), Line
           Masters—Big Book (246)

Word Family: -ig   253

Lesson 1: Objectives (253), Materials (253), Procedure
           (253), "Wacky Wigs" Poem (253), Art Activity
           (254), Conclusion of Lesson (254), Line

Master—"Wacky Wigs" Poem (255), Line Master—Head (256)

Lesson 2: Objectives (257), Materials (257), Procedure (257), "The Big Rig" Poem (257), -ig Blending Strip Activity (258), Challenge Activity (259), Reinforcement Activity (259), Line Master—Pig (260), Flashcards (261)

Lesson 3: Objective (262), Materials (262), Procedure (262), Line Masters—Little Book (263), Line Masters—Big Book (267)

Word Family: -in 274

Lesson 1: Objectives (274), Materials (274), Procedure (274), "My Pinwheel" Poem (274), Art Activity (275), Conclusion of Lesson (275), Line Master—"My Pinwheel" Poem (276), Line Master—Pinwheel (277)

Lesson 2: Objectives (278), Materials (278), Procedure (278), "My Robot" Poem (278), -in Blending Strip Activity (279), Challenge Activity (280), Reinforcement Activity (280), Line Master—Safety Pin (281), Flashcards (282)

Lesson 3: Objective (283), Materials (283), Procedure (283), Line Masters—Little Book (284), Line Masters—Big Book (288)

Word Family: -ine 295

Lesson 1: Objectives (295), Materials (295), Procedure (295), "Sparkle and Shine" Poem (295), Art Activity (296), Conclusion of Lesson (296), Line Master—"Sparkle and Shine" Poem (297), Line Master—Mouth (298)

Lesson 2: Objectives (299), Materials (299), Procedure (299), "A Mighty Fine Swine" Poem (299), -inc Blending Strip Activity (300), Challenge Activity (301), Reinforcement Activity (301), Line Master—Pine (302), Flashcards (303)

Lesson 3: Objective (304), Materials (304), Procedure (304), Line Masters—Little Book (305), Line Masters—Big Book (309)

Word Family: -ip   316

Lesson 1:   Objectives (316), Materials (316), Procedure
(316), "The Crazy Straw" Poem (316), Art
Activity (317), Conclusion of Lesson (317),
Line Master—"The Crazy Straw" Poem (318),
Line Master—Crazy Straw (319)

Lesson 2:   Objectives (320), Materials (320), Procedure
(320), "Eddie the Elephant" Poem (320), -ip
Blending Strip Activity (321), Challenge
Activity (322), Reinforcement Activity (322),
Line Master—Ship (323), Flashcards (324)

Lesson 3:   Objective (325), Materials (325), Procedure
(325), Line Masters—Little Book (326), Line
Masters—Big Book (330)

Word Family: -it   337

Lesson 1:   Objectives (337), Materials (337), Procedure
(337), "Does It Fit?" Poem (337), Art Activity
(338), Conclusion of Lesson (338), Line
Master—"Does It Fit?" Poem (339), Line
Master—Child (340)

Lesson 2:   Objectives (341), Materials (341), Procedure
(341), "How to Make a Banana Split" Poem
(341), -it Blending Strip Activity (342),
Challenge Activity (343), Reinforcement
Activity (343), Line Master—Banana Split
(344), Flashcards (345)

Lesson 3:   Objective (346), Materials (346), Procedure
(346), Line Masters—Little Book (347), Line
Masters—Big Book (351)

Word Family: -og   358

Lesson 1:   Objectives (358), Materials (358), Procedure
(358), "Book Hog" Poem (358), Art Activity
(359), Conclusion of Lesson (359), Line
Master—"Book Hog" Poem (360), Line
Master—Book (361)

Lesson 2:   Objectives (362), Materials (362), Procedure
(362), "Little Frog" Poem (362), -og Blending

Strip Activity (363), Challenge Activity (363), Reinforcement Activity (364), Line Master—Log (365), Flashcards (366)

Lesson 3: Objective (367), Materials (367), Procedure (367), Line Masters—Little Book (368), Line Masters—Big Book (372)

Word Family: -ook 379

Lesson 1: Objectives (379), Materials (379), Procedure (379), "Look!" Poem (379), Art Activity (380), Conclusion of Lesson (380), Line Master—"Look!" Poem (381), Line Master—Mirror (382)

Lesson 2: Objectives (383), Materials (383), Procedure (383), "A Silly Cook" Poem (383), -ook Blending Strip Activity (384), Challenge Activity (385), Reinforcement Activity (385), Line Master—Book (386), Flashcards (387)

Lesson 3: Objective (388), Materials (388), Procedure (388), Line Masters—Little Book (389), Line Masters—Big Book (393)

Word Family: -op 400

Lesson 1: Objectives (400), Materials (400), Procedure (400), "Stop!" Poem (400), Art Activity (401), Conclusion of Lesson (401), Line Master—"Stop!" Poem (402), Line Master—Traffic Light (403)

Lesson 2: Objectives (404), Materials (404), Procedure (404), "The Hippity-Hop" Poem (404), -op Blending Strip Activity (405), Challenge Activity (406), Reinforcement Activity (406), Line Master—Stop Sign (407), Flashcards (408)

Lesson 3: Objective (409), Materials (409), Procedure (409), Line Masters—Little Book (410), Line Masters—Big Book (414)

Word Family: -ot   421

Lesson 1:   Objectives (421), Materials (421), Procedure (421), "My Dog Spot" Poem (421), Art Activity (422), Conclusion of Lesson (422), Line Master—"My Dog Spot" Poem (423), Line Master—Dog (424)

Lesson 2:   Objectives (425), Materials (425), Procedure (425), "The Dot" Poem (425), -ot Blending Strip Activity (426), Challenge Activity (426), Reinforcement Activity (427), Line Master—Pot (428), Flashcards (429)

Lesson 3:   Objective (430), Materials (430), Procedure (430), Line Masters—Little Book (431), Line Masters—Big Book (435)

Word Family: -ug   442

Lesson 1:   Objectives (442), Materials (442), Procedure (442), "Tug of War" Poem (442), Art Activity (443), Conclusion of Lesson (443), Line Master—"Tug of War" Poem (444), Line Master—Children (445)

Lesson 2:   Objectives (446), Materials (446), Procedure (446), "The Smug Bug" Poem (446), -ug Blending Strip Activity (447), Challenge Activity (448), Reinforcement Activity (448), Line Master—Bug (449), Flashcards (450)

Lesson 3:   Objective (451), Materials (451), Procedure (451), Line Masters—Little Book (452), Line Masters—Big Book (456)

Word Family: -ump   463

Lesson 1:   Objectives (463), Materials (463), Procedure (463), "Jump Rope" Poem (463), Art Activity (464), Conclusion of Lesson (464), Line Master—"Jump Rope" Poem (465), Line Master—Children (466)

Lesson 2:   Objectives (467), Materials (467), Procedure (467), "Clara the Camel" Poem (467), -ump Blending Strip Activity (468), Challenge

Activity (469), Reinforcement Activity (469), Line Master—Jump Rope (470), Flashcards (471)

Lesson 3: Objective (472), Materials (472), Procedure (472), Line Masters—Little Book (473), Line Masters—Big Book (477)

Word Family: -un   484

Lesson 1: Objectives (484), Materials (484), Procedure (484), "The Race" Poem (484), Art Activity (485), Conclusion of Lesson (485), Line Master—"The Race" Poem (486), Line Master—Sneaker (487)

Lesson 2: Objectives (488), Materials (488), Procedure (488), "Spinning a Web" Poem (488), -un Blending Strip Activity (489), Challenge Activity (490), Reinforcement Activity (490), Line Master—Sun (491), Flashcards (492)

Lesson 3: Objective (493), Materials (493), Procedure (493), Line Masters—Little Book (494), Line Masters—Big Book (498)

Word Family: -unk   505

Lesson 1: Objectives (505), Materials (505), Procedure (505), "Little Skunk" Poem (505), Art Activity (506), Conclusion of Lesson (506), Line Master—"Little Skunk" Poem (507), Line Master—Skunk (508)

Lesson 2: Objectives (509), Materials (509), Procedure (509), "Slam Dunk!" Poem (509), -unk Blending Strip Activity (510), Challenge Activity (511), Reinforcement Activity (511), Line Master—Skunk (512), Flashcards (513)

Lesson 3: Objective (514), Materials (514), Procedure (514), Line Masters—Little Book (515), Line Masters—Big Book (519)

Word Family
-ake

Lesson 1

Objectives

- To provide exposure and an introduction to the *-ake* word family
- To introduce the anchor word *cake*

Materials

- Chart-sized poem "My Big Cake"
- Chart paper
- Water-based marker

Procedure

1. Read the book *The Cake That Mack Ate* by Rose Robart.
2. Discuss with the children those times when they eat a special cake and what types of cake they like to eat.
3. Tell the children you will now read a poem titled "My Big Cake." Read "My Big Cake" to the children. Model 1:1 by pointing to each word as you read. Invite the children to read through the poem with you the second timc.

My Big Cake

My big cake is as tall as me.
Count the layers—
1-2-3!
The bottom is vanilla,
all creamy and white.
The next layer is chocolate
Hmm . . . dy-no-mite!
Strawberry's last,
all red and sweet.
My big cake . . .
Can't wait to eat!

---

4. Vary this activity by echo reading ("My turn, your turn") and choral reading.

5. Ask the children if they can find the word *cake* in the poem. Invite children to come up and circle the word *cake* with a water-based marker.

6. Now do the art activity with the children, either as a small group or whole class.

Art Activity

Materials

- Scissors
- Crayons
- Line master of poem "My Big Cake"
- Line master of cake
- 12" × 18" yellow construction paper
- Sequins
- Glue
- Stapler

Preparation

Reproduce the poem "My Big Cake" and staple it to the right side of the yellow construction paper.

Procedure

1. Children color the cake. The top layer is red. The middle layer is brown. The bottom layer remains white.

2. Children cut out the cake.

3. Children decorate by gluing sequins on the cake. (*Note:* Carefully supervise the children when working with sequins.)

4. Let dry.

5. Staple the cake to the left side of the poem.

6. Send the poem and art activity home. This gives family members an opportunity to read the poem with the child.

Conclusion of Lesson

Bring children back to the large "My Big Cake" poem. Reread the poem together as a class.

My Big Cake

My big cake is as tall as me.
Count the layers—
1-2-3!
The bottom is vanilla,
all creamy and white.
The next layer is chocolate
Hmm . . . dy-no-mite!
Strawberry's last,
all red and sweet.
My big cake . . .
Can't wait to eat!

- -

My Big Cake

My big cake is as tall as me.
Count the layers—
1-2-3!
The bottom is vanilla,
all creamy and white.
The next layer is chocolate
Hmm . . . dy-no-mite!
Strawberry's last,
all red and sweet.
My big cake . . .
Can't wait to eat!

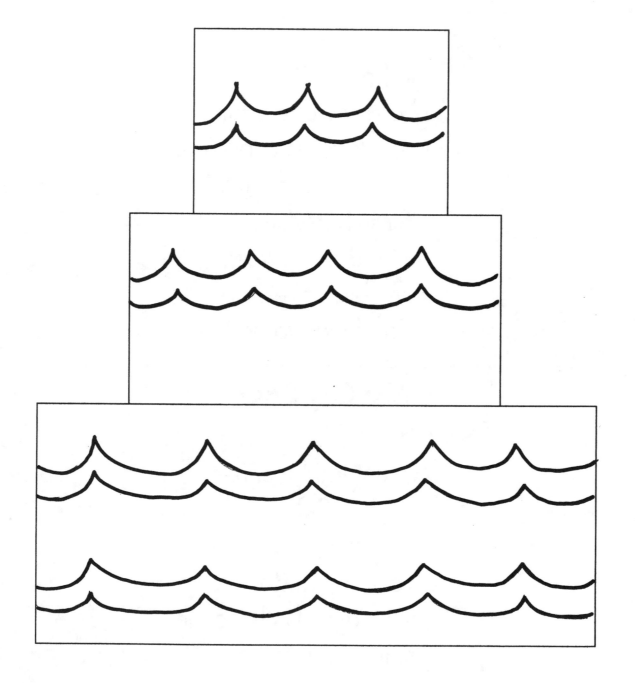

LINE MASTER—CAKE

Lesson 2

Objectives

- Child will recognize *-ake* words visually and auditorily.
- Child will read words that belong in the *-ake* word family.

Materials

- Large copy of poem "Jake the Snake"
- Teacher-made model of the *-ake* blending strip
- Water-based marker

Procedure

1. Show children the poem "Jake the Snake."

Jake the Snake

Jake and his friend lived down by the lake.
They would slither and slide and make their tails shake.
Each day they would take a trip around the lake
to see the lady with the rake.
"Hey, lady with the rake!" shouted Jake the snake.
"You said you'd bake us a cornflake cake!"
"Okay!" said the lady with the rake.
"Today I will make your cornflake cake."
"Hurray!" said Jake and his friend the other snake.
With that their tails began to shake.
Quickly they slithered back around the lake.
"Too quick! Slow down, for goodness sake!
My friend," said Jake the snake, "put on the brake!"
Along came the lady with the rake.
"Here is your delicious cornflake cake!"
"Thanks!" said Jake and his friend the other snake.

---

2. Tell the children they are going to hear a poem about two silly snakes.
3. Read the poem to the children.
4. Ask children what they notice about the poem.
5. Read the poem again. This time emphasize the rhyming words.
6. Remind the children that words that sound alike at the end are called rhyming words.

7. Read the poem again and have the children listen for the words that rhyme. Have the children give you a "thumbs up" (or some other "secret signal") when they hear a rhyming word.

8. Circle with the water-based marker each rhyming word as it is read.

9. Read all the circled words aloud.

10. Write the circled rhyming words from the poem in a column on a separate piece of chart paper.

11. Ask the children what they notice that is the same about the words. Anything different?

12. Show the children that the only difference in each -*ake* word is the beginning sound. The middle and ending sounds are the same.

13. Ask the children for other words in the -*ake* word family.

14. Show the children the -*ake* blending strip and snake. Say "ake" out loud. Tell the children you will now show them words that belong to the -*ake* word family.

15. Move the blending strip to create all the -*ake* word-family words. Say the words as you create them. Have the children repeat them after you. Repeat this activity several times.

16. Explain to the children they will make their own -*ake* blending strip.

-ake Blending Strip Activity

Materials

- Line master of snake
- Blending strip with letters: *m, b, c, r, t, f, l, w, s, J, sh, sn, br* (You may edit the letters on the strip.)
- Blank writing paper
- Line master of -*ake* word family flashcards
- Crayons
- Scissors

Procedure

1. Give children the line master of the snake, scissors, and crayons.
2. Children color in the snake.
3. Children cut out the snake.
4. Cut two 1-inch vertical slits to the left of the chunk printed on the blending strip. Be sure to leave a 1-inch space between the slits.
5. Slide the strip through the slits.

6. Children read all the *-ake* words to you by sliding the strip through the snake.

7. Vary the activity by having children read to a partner, you, or any other adult.

8. Children then write all the words on the writing paper provided.

9. Send the blending strip and flashcards home to reinforce the *-ake* word family.

Challenge Activity

Children will turn the writing paper over and use each *-ake* word in a sentence. They can also make up a silly poem of their own using some or all of the *-ake* words.

Reinforcement Activity

1. For a small group mini-lesson, put the magnetic letters **c a k e** on an overhead projector (or on the floor facing the children if you do not have an overhead).

2. Tell children they know the word *cake.*

3. Run your finger under the word *cake* and say *c-a-k-e,* stretching out the word as you say it. Again, slide your finger under the word *cake* and stretch it out. Have children say it with you this time.

4. Remove the "c" from the word and tell children this chunk of the word is *ake.*

5. Put an "m" in front of the *-ake* on the overhead. Again, slide your finger under the word, stretching out *m-a-k-e* as you say it. Repeat this procedure with the letters *b, r, t, f, w, l, s, J, sh, sn, br.*

6. Have the children practice making *-ake* family words individually or with a partner using the magnetic letters as you demonstrated on the overhead projector.

ake

LINE MASTER—SNAKE BLENDING STRIP

make	bake
cake	lake
rake	take
shake	snake

Lesson 3

Objective

- Child will read -*ake* words in the context of a story.

Materials

- Big Book *Jake the Snake*
- Little Book *Jake the Snake*
- Crayons

Procedure

1. Introduce the Big Book *Jake the Snake*. Read the title to the children.

2. Remind the children they have been learning about the -*ake* word family. Elicit words from the -*ake* word family before you begin.

3. Take a picture walk through the book. Label all the pictures. Tell the children what is happening using some of the text from the book.

4. Read the book to the children, modeling 1:1, directionality, and return sweep.

5. Reread the book, inviting the children to read along with you. Do this several times. You can vary the activity by echo reading or choral reading.

6. Give the children their own copy of the book. Ask them to read the book to themselves and then color in all the pictures. Have them read the book to a partner.

7. Listen to the children read the book independently or send the books home as a "read together," depending on the reading ability of each child.

Jake the Snake

Name _____

Jake and his friend lived down by the lake. They would slither and slide and make their tails shake.

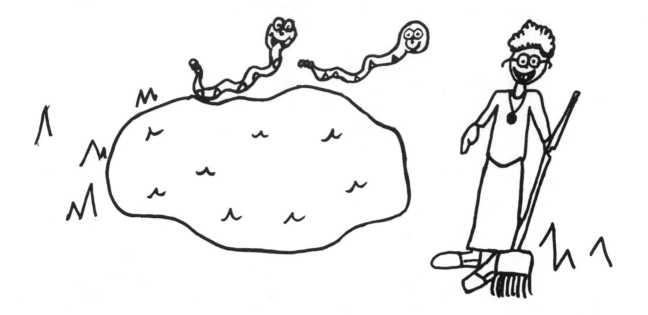

Each day they would take a trip around the lake
to see the lady with the rake.

- -

"Hey, lady with the rake!" shouted Jake the snake.
"You said you'd bake us a cornflake cake!"
"Okay!" said the lady with the rake.
"Today I will make your cornflake cake."

"Hurray!" said Jake and his friend the other snake.
With that their tails began to shake.
Quickly they slithered back around the lake.

- -

"Too quick! Slow down, for goodness sake! My
friend," said Jake the snake, "put on the brake!"

Along came the lady with the rake.
"Here is your delicious cornflake cake!"

- -

"Thanks!" said Jake and his friend the other snake.

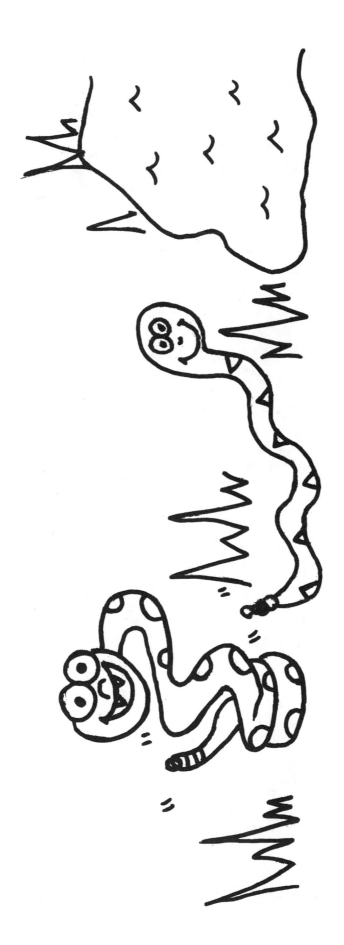

LINE MASTER—"JAKE THE SNAKE" BIG BOOK

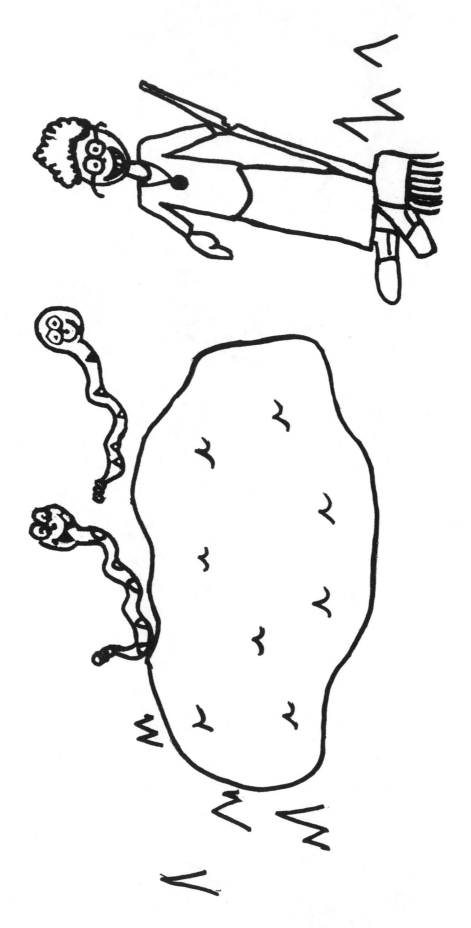

LINE MASTER—"JAKE THE SNAKE" BIG BOOK

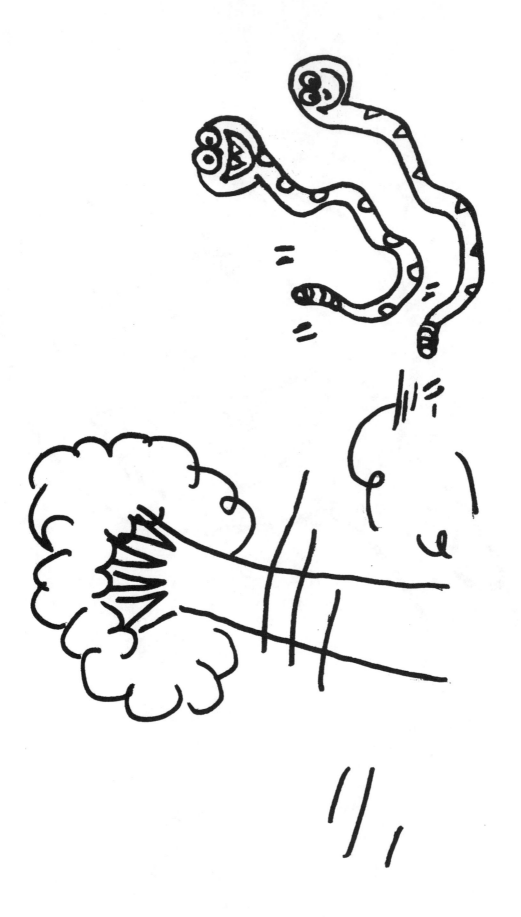

LINE MASTER—"JAKE THE SNAKE" BIG BOOK

LINE MASTER—"JAKE THE SNAKE" BIG BOOK

LINE MASTER—"JAKE THE SNAKE" BIG BOOK

LINE MASTER—"JAKE THE SNAKE" BIG BOOK

Word Family

-am

Lesson 1

Objectives

- To provide exposure and an introduction to the -am word family
- To introduce the anchor word am

Materials

- Chart-sized poem "I Am!"
- Chart paper
- Hand-held mirror
- Water-based marker

Procedure

1. Read and discuss the book *We Are All Alike . . . We Are All Different* written and illustrated by the Cheltenham Elementary School Kindergartners.

2. Talk to the children about what makes each of them special. Emphasize attributes such as curly hair, straight hair, brown eyes, blue eyes, tan skin, olive skin, etc.

3. Allow each child the opportunity to look in the hand-held mirror. Remind children to pay attention to the attributes that make each one of them unique.

4. Tell the children you will now read a poem titled "I Am!" Read "I Am!" to the children. Model 1:1 by pointing to each word as you read. Invite the children to read through the poem with you the second time.

I Am!

I am big.
I am small.
I am either short or tall.
I am smart and lots of fun.
No one's quite like me—
I'm the only one!

---

5. Vary this activity by echo reading ("My turn, your turn") and choral reading.

6. Ask the children if they can find the word *am* in the poem. Invite children to come up and circle the word *am* with a water-based marker.

7. Now do the art activity with the children, either as a small group or whole class.

Art Activity

Materials

- Multicultural crayons
- Crayons
- Line master of poem "I Am!"
- Line master of border
- 12" × 18" blue construction paper
- Hand-held mirror
- Stapler

Preparation

Reproduce the poem "I Am!" and staple it to the right side of the blue construction paper.

Procedure

1. Children draw their face inside the border.
2. Staple the self-portrait to the left side of the poem.
3. Send the poem and art activity home. This gives family members an opportunity to read the poem with the child.

Conclusion of Lesson

Bring children back to the large "I Am!" poem. Reread the poem together as a class.

I Am!

I am big.
I am small.
I am either short or tall.
I am smart and lots of fun.
No one's quite like me—
I'm the only one!

I Am!

I am big.
I am small.
I am either short or tall.
I am smart and lots of fun.
No one's quite like me—
I'm the only one!

LINE MASTER—"I AM" POEM

I Am!

Lesson 2

Objectives

- Child will recognize *-am* words visually and auditorily.
- Child will read words that belong in the *-am* word family.

Materials

- Large copy of poem "Picnic at the Dam"
- Teacher-made model of the *-am* blending strip
- Water-based marker

Procedure

1. Show children the poem "Picnic at the Dam."

Picnic at the Dam

"Do you like baseball?" said Pam to Sam.
"Sure," said Sam. "I play at the field down by the dam.
When I hit the ball hard, it goes . . . WHAM!
When I hit the ball hard, it goes . . . SLAM!
Baseball talk makes me hungry!" said Sam to Pam.
"I have a sandwich. Would you like some ham?" asked Pam.
"No, thanks, I've got bread and jam," replied Sam.
So Sam and Pam had a picnic at the dam.
They feasted on their ham and jam.

---

2. Tell children they are going to hear a poem about Pam and Sam who had a picnic at the dam.
3. Read the poem to the children.
4. Ask children what they notice about the poem.
5. Read the poem again. This time emphasize the rhyming words.
6. Remind the children that words that sound alike at the end are called rhyming words.
7. Read the poem again and have the children listen for the words that rhyme. Have the children give you a "thumbs up" (or some other "secret signal") when they hear a rhyming word.
8. Circle with the water-based marker each rhyming word as it is read.
9. Read all the circled words aloud.
10. Write the circled rhyming words from the poem in a column on a separate piece of chart paper.

11. Ask the children what they notice that is the same about the words. Anything different?

12. Show the children that the only difference in each -am word is the beginning sound. The middle and ending sounds are the same.

13. Ask the children for other words in the -am word family.

14. Show the children the -am blending strip and jar of jam. Say "am" out loud. Tell the children you will now show them words that belong to the -am word family.

15. Move the blending strip to create all the -am word-family words. Say the words as you create them. Have the children repeat them after you. Repeat this activity several times.

16. Explain to the children they will make their own -am blending strip.

-am Blending Strip Activity

Materials

- Line master of jar of jam
- Blending strip with letters: *d, j, b, r, h, P, S, wh, sl, sw* (You may edit the letters on the strip.)
- Blank writing paper
- Line master of -am word family flashcards
- Crayons
- Scissors

Procedure

1. Give children the line master of the jar of jam, scissors, and crayons.

2. Children color in the jar of jam.

3. Children cut out the jar of jam.

4. Cut two 1-inch vertical slits to the left of the chunk printed on the blending strip. Be sure to leave a 1-inch space between the slits.

5. Slide the strip through the slits.

6. Children read all the -am words to you by sliding the strip through the jar of jam.

7. Vary the activity by having children read to a partner, you, or any other adult.

8. Children then write all the words on the writing paper provided.

9. Send the blending strip and flashcards home to reinforce the -am word family.

Challenge Activity

Children will turn the writing paper over and use each -*am* word in a sentence. They can also make up a silly poem of their own using some or all of the -*am* words.

Reinforcement Activity

1. For a small group mini-lesson, put the magnetic letters **j a m** on an overhead projector (or on the floor facing the children if you do not have an overhead).

2. Tell children they know the word *jam.*

3. Run your finger under the word *jam* and say *j-a-m,* stretching out the word as you say it. Again, slide your finger under the word *jam* and stretch it out. Have children say it with you this time.

4. Remove the "j" from the word and tell children this chunk of the word is *am.*

5. Put an "h" in front of the -*am* on the overhead. Again, slide your finger under the word, stretching out *h-a-m* as you say it. Repeat this procedure with the letters *d, b, r, P, S, wh, sl, tr, cl, sh, sw, cr.*

6. Have the children practice making -am family words individually or with a partner using the magnetic letters as you demonstrated on the overhead projector.

LINE MASTER—JAM JAR BLENDING STRIP

dam	jam
ham	ram
Pam	Sam
swam	slam

Lesson 3

Objective

- Child will read -am words in the context of a story.

Materials

- Big Book *Picnic at the Dam*
- Little Book *Picnic at the Dam*
- Crayons

Procedure

1. Introduce the Big Book *Picnic at the Dam*. Read the title to the children.

2. Remind the children they have been learning about the -am word family. Elicit words from the -am word family before you begin.

3. Take a picture walk through the book. Label all the pictures. Tell the children what is happening using some of the text from the book.

4. Read the book to the children, modeling 1:1, directionality, and return sweep.

5. Reread the book, inviting the children to read along with you. Do this several times. You can vary the activity by echo reading or choral reading.

6. Give the children their own copy of the book. Have them read the book to themselves and then color in all the pictures. Have them read the book to a partner.

7. Listen to the children read the book independently or send the books home as a "read together," depending on the reading ability of each child.

Picnic at the Dam

Name _____

- -

"Do you like baseball?" said Pam to Sam.

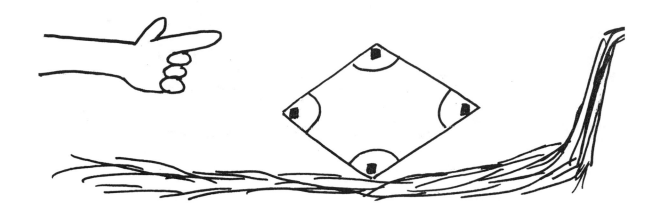

"Sure," said Sam. "I play at the field
down by the dam."

- -

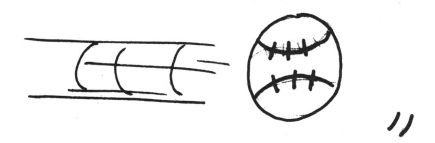

"When I hit the ball hard, it goes . . . WHAM!"

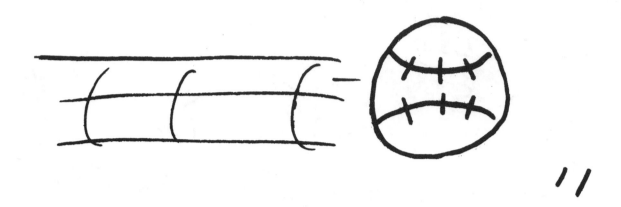

"When I hit the ball hard, it goes . . . SLAM!"

"Baseball talk makes me hungry!"
said Sam to Pam.

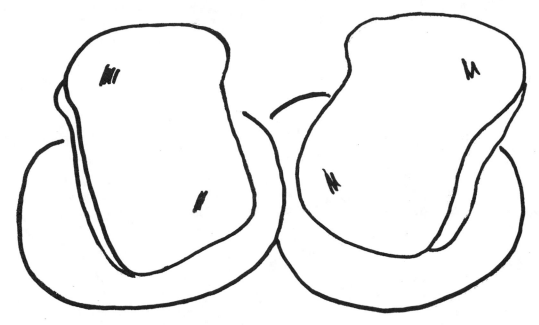

"I have a sandwich. Would you like some ham?"
asked Pam.
"No, thanks. I've got bread and jam," replied Sam.

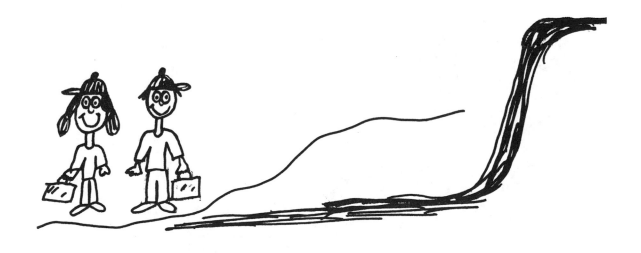

So Sam and Pam had a picnic at the dam.
They feasted on their ham and jam.

LINE MASTER—"PICNIC AT THE DAM" BIG BOOK

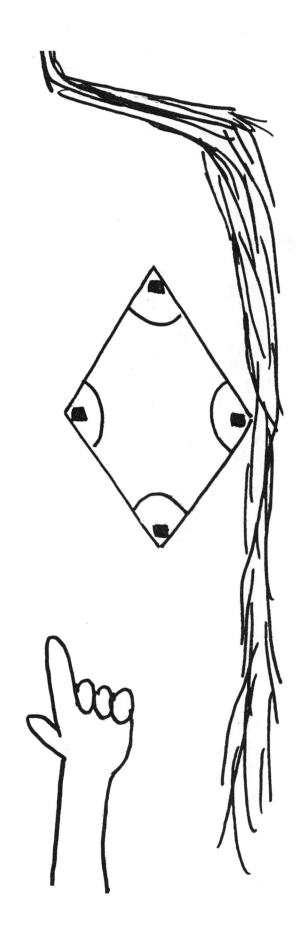

LINE MASTER—"PICNIC AT THE DAM" BIG BOOK

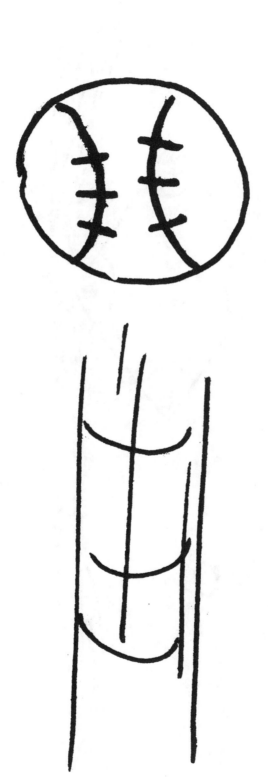

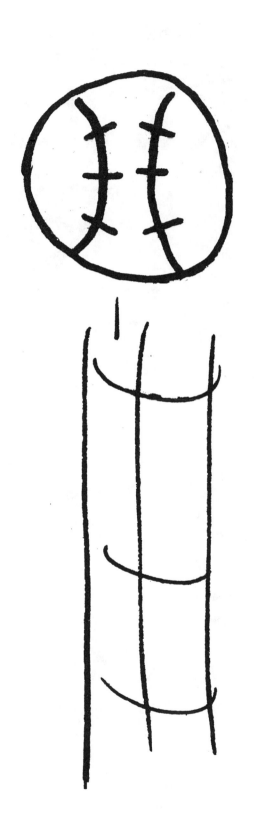

LINE MASTER—"PICNIC AT THE DAM" BIG BOOK

LINE MASTER—"PICNIC AT THE DAM" BIG BOOK

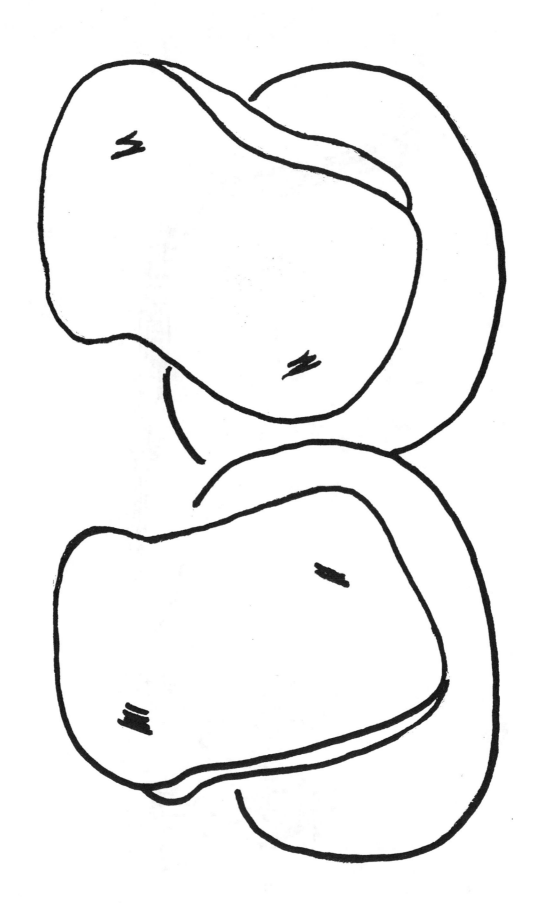

LINE MASTER—"PICNIC AT THE DAM" BIG BOOK

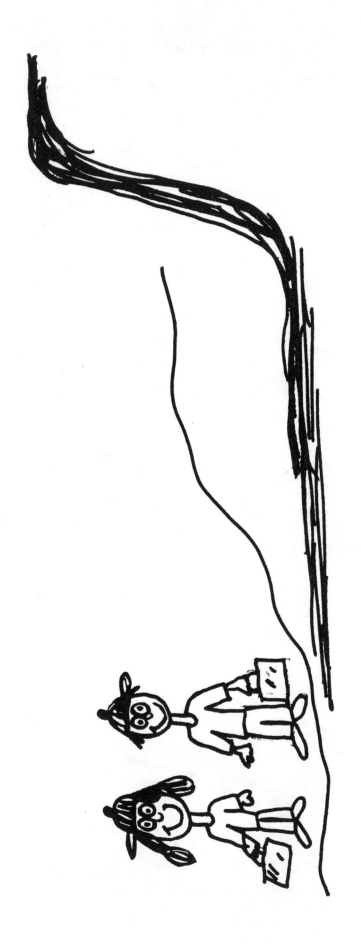

LINE MASTER—"PICNIC AT THE DAM" BIG BOOK

-ame

Lesson 1

Objectives

- To provide exposure and an introduction to the *-ame* word family
- To introduce the anchor word *games*

Materials

- Chart-sized poem "Games"
- Chart paper
- Water-based marker

Procedure

1. Brainstorm with the children all the different types of games they play. (Include board games, team games, ball games, etc.) This will activate prior knowledge and fill in gaps for children. List all responses on a piece of chart paper or chalkboard. You can also use a graphic organizer, such as the web shown here.

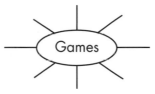

2. Tell the children you will now read a poem titled "Games." Read "Games" to the children. Model 1:1 by pointing to each word as you read. Invite the children to read through the poem with you the second time.

> **Games**
>
> I like to play games.
> Games are lots of fun.
> There are board games and card games,
> something for everyone!
> Running games and ball games
> are fun to play, too . . .
> I love to play games!
> Don't you?

3. Vary this activity by echo reading ("My turn, your turn") and choral reading.
4. Ask the children if they can find the word *games* in the poem. Invite children to come up and circle the word *games* with a water-based marker.
5. Now do the art activity with the children, either as a small group or whole class.

Art Activity

Materials

- Pencils
- Line master of poem "Games"
- Line master of board game
- 12" × 18" orange construction paper
- Crayons
- Stapler

Preparation

Reproduce the poem "Games" and staple it to the right side of the orange construction paper.

Procedure

1. Children complete the following sentence: My favorite game to play is _____ because _____. (*Note:* Take dictation if necessary.)
2. Children color the squares of the gameboard.
3. Staple the board game to the left side of the poem.
4. Send the poem and art activity home. This gives family members an opportunity to read the poem with the child.

Conclusion of Lesson

Bring children back to the large "Games" poem. Reread the poem together as a class.

Games

I like to play games.
Games are lots of fun.
There are board games and card games,
something for everyone!
Running games and ball games
are fun to play, too . . .
I love to play games!
Don't you?

- -

Games

I like to play games.
Games are lots of fun.
There are board games and card games,
something for everyone!
Running games and ball games
are fun to play, too . . .
I love to play games!
Don't you?

| Start | | | Move ahead 3 spaces. | | | Move back 2 spaces. |

Take another turn!

Move back 1 space.

Pick a card.

Lose a turn.

My favorite game to play is

_____

because

_____

_____ .

Roll the dice.

Skip a turn!

Finish!

Lesson 2

Objectives

- Child will recognize -ame words visually and auditorily.
- Child will read words that belong in the -ame word family.

Materials

- Large copy of poem "The Word Game (A Rap)"
- Teacher-made model of the -ame blending strip
- Water-based marker

Procedure

1. Show children the poem "The Word Game."

The Word Game (A Rap)
Come on, everybody! Let's play the word game.
You start with a chunk that stays the same.
Add a new letter to play the game.
Start with "-ame," then add a "c"—the new word's "came."
(That's easy for me!)
Now try "n"—"ame" stays the same. The new word's "name."
(I like this game!)
That's too tame! Let's add some blends like
flame, shame, blame!
Come on, everybody! Let's play the word game.

---

2. Tell the children they are going to hear a funny poem about a word game.
3. Read the poem to the children.
4. Ask children what they notice about the poem.
5. Read the poem again. This time emphasize the rhyming words.
6. Remind the children that words that sound alike at the end are called rhyming words.
7. Read the poem again and have the children listen for the words that rhyme. Have the children give you a "thumbs up" (or some other "secret signal") when they hear a rhyming word.
8. Circle with the water-based marker each rhyming word as it is read.
9. Read all the circled words aloud.
10. Write the circled rhyming words from the poem in a column on a separate piece of chart paper.

11. Ask the children what they notice that is the same about the words. Anything different?

12. Show the children that the only difference in each -*ame* word is the beginning sound. The middle and ending sounds are the same.

13. Ask the children for other words in the -*ame* word family.

14. Show the children the -*ame* blending strip and frame. Say "ame" out loud. Tell the children you will now show them words that belong to the -*ame* word family.

15. Move the blending strip to create all the -*ame* word-family words. Say the words as you create them. Have the children repeat them after you. Repeat this activity several times.

16. Explain to the children they will make their own -*ame* blending strip.

-ame Blending Strip Activity

Materials

- Line master of frame
- Blending strip with letters: *s, n, g, l, c, t, m, f, bl, fr, fl, sh* (You may edit the letters on the strip.)
- Blank writing paper
- Line master of -*ame* word family flashcards
- Crayons
- Scissors

Procedure

1. Give children the line master of the frame, scissors, and crayons.
2. Children color in the frame.
3. Children cut out the frame.
4. Cut two 1-inch vertical slits to the left of the chunk printed on the blending strip. Be sure to leave a 1-inch space between the slits.
5. Slide the strip through the slits.
6. Children read all the -*ame* words to you by sliding the strip through the frame.
7. Vary the activity by having children read to a partner, you, or any other adult.
8. Children then write all the words on the writing paper provided.
9. Send the blending strip and flashcards home to reinforce the -*ame* word family.

Challenge Activity

Children will turn the writing paper over and use each -ame word in a sentence. They can also make up a silly poem of their own using some or all of the -ame words.

Reinforcement Activity

1. For a small group mini-lesson, put the magnetic letters **g a m e** on an overhead projector (or on the floor facing the children if you do not have an overhead).

2. Tell children they know the word *game*.

3. Run your finger under the word *game* and say *g-a-m-e*, stretching out the word as you say it. Again, slide your finger under the word *game* and stretch it out. Have children say it with you this time.

4. Remove the "g" from the word and tell children this chunk of the word is *ame*.

5. Put an "n" in front of the -ame on the overhead. Again, slide your finger under the word, stretching out *n-a-m-e* as you say it. Repeat this procedure with the letters *s, l, c, t, f, bl, fr, fl, sh*. Have the children practice making -ame family words individually or with a partner using the magnetic letters as you demonstrated on the overhead projector.

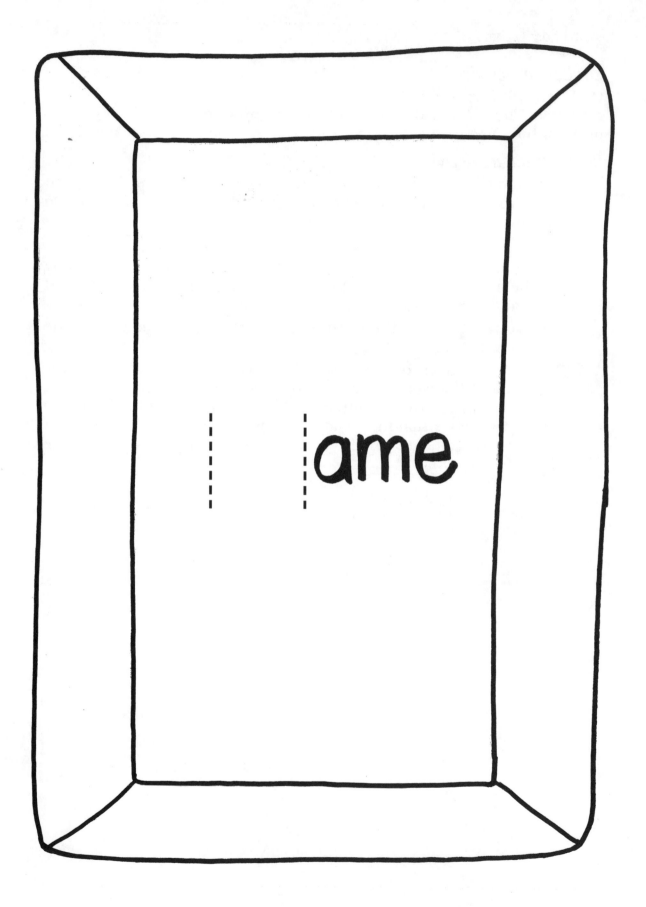

ame

LINE MASTER—FRAME BLENDING STRIP

game	same
fame	name
blame	tame
came	shame

LINE MASTER—*AME* WORD FAMILY FLASHCARDS

Lesson 3

Objective

- Child will read -ame words in the context of a story.

Materials

- Big Book *The Word Game (A Rap)*
- Little Book *The Word Game (A Rap)*
- Crayons

Procedure

1. Introduce the Big Book *The Word Game*. Read the title to the children.

2. Remind the children they have been learning about the -ame word family. Elicit words from the -ame word family before you begin.

3. Take a picture walk through the book. Label all the pictures. Tell the children what is happening using some of the text from the book.

4. Read the book to the children, modeling 1:1, directionality, and return sweep.

5. Reread the book, inviting the children to read along with you. Do this several times. You can vary the activity by echo reading or choral reading.

6. Give the children their own copy of the book. Have them read the book to themselves and then color in all the pictures. Have them read the book to a partner.

7. Listen to the children read the book independently or send the books home as a "read together," depending on the reading ability of each child.

The Word Game
(A Rap)

Name _____

- -

Come on, everybody! Let's play the word game.

You start with a chunk that stays the same.
Add a new letter to play the game.

C - ame

Start with "ame," then add a "c"—
the new word's "came." (That's easy for me!)

Now try "n"—"ame" stays the same.
The new word's "name." (I like this game!)

That's too tame! Let's add some blends
like flame, shame, blame!

Come on, EVERYBODY!

- -

ame
came
name
flame
shame
blame

Let's play the word game!

LINE MASTER—"THE WORD GAME" BIG BOOK

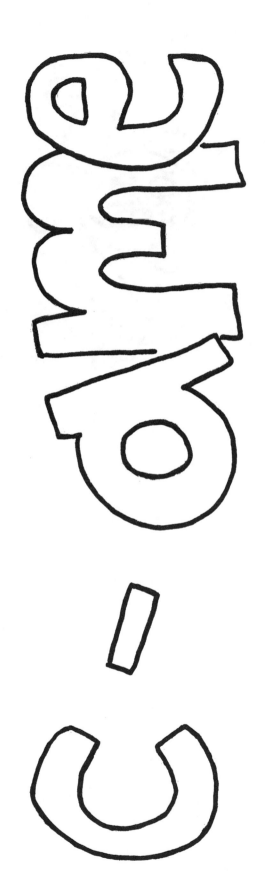

LINE MASTER—"THE WORD GAME" BIG BOOK

LINE MASTER—"THE WORD GAME" BIG BOOK

LINE MASTER—"THE WORD GAME" BIG BOOK

ame

came
name
flame
shame
blame

LINE MASTER—"THE WORD GAME" BIG BOOK

Word Family

-an

Lesson 1

Objectives

- To provide exposure and an introduction to the *-an* word family
- To introduce the anchor word *can*

Materials

- Chart-sized poem "I Can!"
- Chart paper
- Water-based marker

Procedure

1. Brainstorm with children all the things they can do. This will activate prior knowledge and fill in gaps for children. List all responses on a piece of chart paper or chalkboard. You can also use a graphic organizer, such as the web shown here.

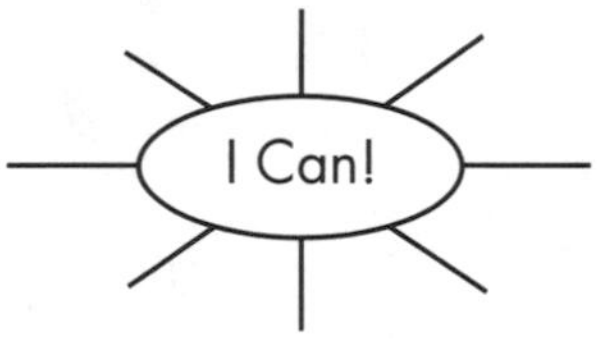

2. Tell the children you will now read a poem titled "I Can!" Read "I Can!" to the children. Model 1:1 by pointing to each word as you read. Invite the children to read through the poem with you the second time.

I Can!

I can dance.
I can sing.
I can do most
anything!
I can read.
I can write.
Look at me—
I'm out of sight!

3. Vary this activity by echo reading ("My turn, your turn") and choral reading.

4. Ask the children if they can find the word *can* in the poem. Invite children to come up and circle the word *can* with a water-based marker.

5. Now do the art activity with the children, either as a small group or whole class.

Art Activity

Materials
- Scissors
- Crayons
- Line master of poem "I Can!"
- Line master of "I Can" border
- 12" × 18" yellow construction paper
- Stapler

Preparation
Reproduce the poem "I Can!" and staple it to the right side of the yellow construction paper.

Procedure
1. Children draw a picture of something they can do on the "I Can" line master paper.
2. Children will complete the sentence: I can _____.
3. Children color in the border.
4. Staple the "I can" paper on the left side of the poem.
5. Send the poem and art activity home. This gives family members an opportunity to read the poem with the child.

Conclusion of Lesson

Bring children back to the large "I Can!" poem. Reread the poem together as a class.

I **Can!**

I can dance.
I can sing.
I can do most
anything!
I can read.
I can write.
Look at me—
I'm out of sight!

I **Can!**

I can dance.
I can sing.
I can do most
anything!
I can read.
I can write.
Look at me—
I'm out of sight!

I can..._____

_____

LINE MASTER—"I CAN" BORDER

Lesson 2

Objectives
- Child will recognize *-an* words visually and auditorily.
- Child will read words that belong in the *-an* word family.

Materials
- Large copy of poem "Stan and Jan"
- Teacher-made model of the *-an* blending strip
- Water-based marker

Procedure
1. Show children the poem "Stan and Jan."

> **Stan and Jan**
>
> Have you met Stan and his friend Jan?
> They read and read wherever they can.
> They read in the house and by the fan.
> They read in the car and in the van.
> They took their books and ran and ran.
> They ran to read to their friend Dan.
> "I have a plan!" said their friend Dan.
> "Let's **all** read together whenever we can."

2. Tell the children they are going to hear a poem about Stan and Jan who love to read.
3. Read the poem to the children.
4. Ask children what they notice about the poem.
5. Read the poem again. This time emphasize the rhyming words.
6. Remind the children that words that sound alike at the end are called rhyming words.
7. Read the poem again and have the children listen for the words that rhyme. Have the children give you a "thumbs up" (or some other "secret signal") when they hear a rhyming word.
8. Circle with the water-based marker each rhyming word as it is read.
9. Read all the circled words aloud.
10. Write the circled rhyming words from the poem in a column on a separate piece of chart paper.

11. Ask the children what they notice the same about the words. Anything different?

12. Show the children that the only difference in each *-an* word is the beginning sound. The middle and ending sounds are the same.

13. Ask the children for other words in the *-an* word family.

14. Show the children the *-an* blending strip and can. Say "an" out loud. Tell the children you will now show them words that belong to the *-an* word family.

15. Move the blending strip to create all the *-an* word-family words. Say the words as you create them. Have the children repeat them after you. Repeat this activity several times.

16. Explain to the children they will make their own *-an* blending strip.

-an Blending Strip Activity

Materials

- Line master of can
- Blending strip with letters: *t, c, D, m, p, f, r, b, v, N, J, St, Fr, pl, th* (You may edit the letters on the strip.)
- Blank writing paper
- Line master of *-an* word family flashcards
- Crayons
- Scissors

Procedure

1. Give children the line master of the can, scissors, and crayons.
2. Children color in the can.
3. Children cut out the can.
4. Cut two 1-inch vertical slits to the left of the chunk printed on the blending strip. Be sure to leave a 1-inch space between the slits.
5. Slide the strip through the slits.
6. Children read all the *-an* words to you by sliding the strip through the can.
7. Vary the activity by having children read to a partner, you, or any other adult.
8. Children then write all the words on the writing paper provided.
9. Send the blending strip and flashcards home to reinforce the *-an* word family.

Challenge Activity

Children will turn the writing paper over and use each -an word in a sentence. They can also make up a silly poem of their own using some or all of the -an words.

Reinforcement Activity

1. For a small group mini-lesson, put the magnetic letters **c a n** on an overhead projector (or on the floor facing the children if you do not have an overhead).

2. Tell children they know the word can.

3. Run your finger under the word can and say c-a-n, stretching out the word as you say it. Again, slide your finger under the word can and stretch it out. Have children say it with you this time.

4. Remove the "c" from the word and tell children this chunk of the word is an.

5. Put a "t" in front of the -an on the overhead. Again, slide your finger under the word, stretching out t-a-n as you say it. Repeat this procedure with the letters D, m, p, f, r, b, v, N, J, St, Fr, pl, th.

6. Have the children practice making -an family words individually or with a partner using the magnetic letters as you demonstrated on the overhead projector.

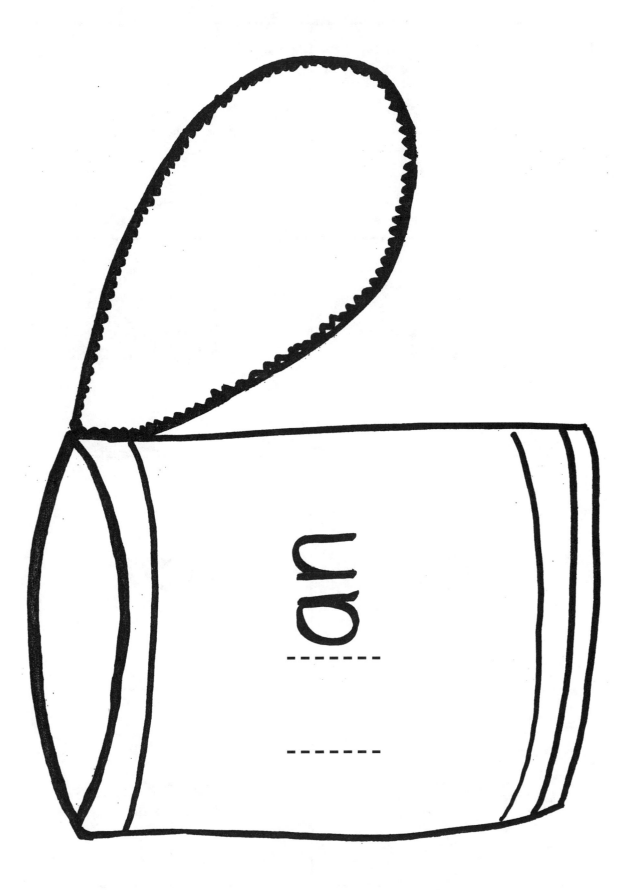

an

LINE MASTER—CAN BLENDING STRIP

can	man
pan	fan
ran	van
plan	tan

Lesson 3

Objective

- Child will read -*an* words in the context of a story.

Materials

- Big Book *Stan and Jan*
- Little Book *Stan and Jan*
- Crayons

Procedure

1. Introduce the Big Book *Stan and Jan*. Read the title to the children.
2. Remind the children they have been learning about the -*an* word family. Elicit words from the -*an* word family before you begin.
3. Take a picture walk through the book. Label all the pictures. Tell the children what is happening using some of the text from the book.
4. Read the book to the children, modeling 1:1, directionality, and return sweep.
5. Reread the book, inviting the children to read along with you. Do this several times. You can vary the activity by echo reading or choral reading.
6. Give the children their own copy of the book. Have them read the book to themselves and then color in all the pictures. Have them read the book to a partner.
7. Listen to the children read the book independently or send the books home as a "read together," depending on the reading ability of each child.

Stan and Jan

Name _____

Have you met Stan and his friend Jan?
They read and read wherever they can.

They read in the house and by the fan.

They read in the car and in the van.

LINE MASTER—"STAN AND JAN" LITTLE BOOK

They took their books and ran and ran.

They ran to read to their friend Dan.

"I have a plan!" said their friend Dan.

- -

"Let's **all** read together whenever we can."

LINE MASTER—"STAN AND JAN" BIG BOOK

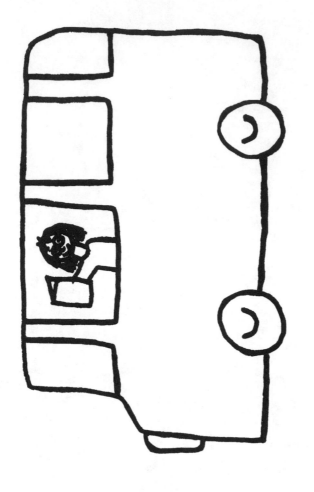

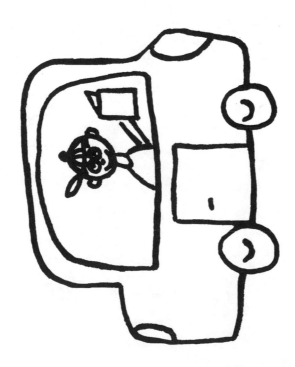

LINE MASTER—"STAN AND JAN" BIG BOOK

LINE MASTER—"STAN AND JAN" BIG BOOK

LINE MASTER—"STAN AND JAN" BIG BOOK

LINE MASTER—"STAN AND JAN" BIG BOOK

LINE MASTER—"STAN AND JAN" BIG BOOK

Word Family

-at

Lesson 1

Objectives

- To provide exposure and an introduction to the *-at* word family
- To introduce the anchor word *cat*

Materials

- Chart-sized poem "Cats, Cats, Cats"
- Chart paper
- Water-based marker

Procedure

1. Brainstorm with the children things they know about cats. This will activate prior knowledge and fill in gaps for children. List all responses on a piece of chart paper or chalkboard. You can also use a graphic organizer, such as the web shown here.

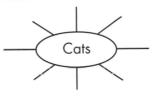

2. Tell the children you will now read a poem titled "Cats, Cats, Cats." Read "Cats, Cats, Cats" to the children. Model 1:1 by pointing to each word as you read. Invite the children to read through the poem with you the second time.

Cats, Cats, Cats

A lion is a cat.
A tiger is a cat.
A leopard is a cat.
Can you imagine that?
Cats with stripes.
Cats with spots.
Cats are pets to love a lot!

3. Vary this activity by echo reading ("My turn, your turn") and choral reading.

4. Ask the children if they can find the word *cat* in the poem. Invite children to come up and circle the word *cat* with a water-based marker.

5. Now do the art activity with the children, either as a small group or whole class.

Art Activity

Materials

- Scissors
- Line master of poem "Cats, Cats, Cats"
- Line master of cat face
- 12" × 18" green construction paper
- Multicolored chenille stems or pipe cleaners (two per child)
- Markers
- Stapler

Preparation

Reproduce the poem "Cats, Cats, Cats" and staple it to the right side of the green construction paper.

Procedure

1. Children draw a face on the line master of the cat with markers.
2. Children cut out the cat's face.
3. You push the chenille stems or pipe cleaners through the cat's face to make the whiskers.
4. Staple the cat's face to the left side of the poem.
5. Send the poem and art activity home. This gives family members an opportunity to read the poem with the child.

Conclusion of Lesson

Bring children back to the large "Cats, Cats, Cats" poem. Reread the poem together as a class.

Cats, Cats, Cats

A lion is a cat.

A tiger is a cat.

A leopard is a cat.

Can you imagine that?

Cats with stripes.

Cats with spots.

Cats are pets to love a lot!

- -

Cats, Cats, Cats

A lion is a cat.

A tiger is a cat.

A leopard is a cat.

Can you imagine that?

Cats with stripes.

Cats with spots.

Cats are pets to love a lot!

LINE MASTER—"CATS, CATS, CATS" POEM

LINE MASTER—CAT

Lesson 2

Objectives

- Child will recognize -at words visually and auditorily.
- Child will read words that belong in the -at word family.

Materials

- Large copy of poem "Pat the Fat Cat"
- Teacher-made model of the -at blending strip
- Water-based marker

Procedure

1. Show children the poem "Pat the Fat Cat."

Pat the Fat Cat

Pat the fat cat got a brand new hat.
"Wow!" He liked how he looked in his new hat.
"Hey, Nat!" said Pat the fat cat. "Do you like my new hat?"
"I **like** that hat!" said Nat the rat. "Can I try it?"
"Sit on the mat and try my new hat."
Nat sat on the mat and tried the hat . . .
"Oh, drat!"

---

2. Tell children they are going to hear a poem about a fat cat named Pat who got a new hat.
3. Read the poem to the children.
4. Ask children what they notice about the poem.
5. Read the poem again. This time emphasize the rhyming words.
6. Remind the children that words that sound alike at the end are called rhyming words.
7. You read the poem again and have the children listen for the words that rhyme. Have the children give you a "thumbs up" (or some other "secret signal") when they hear a rhyming word.
8. Circle with the water-based marker each rhyming word as it is read.
9. Read all the circled words aloud.
10. Write the circled rhyming words from the poem in a column on a separate piece of chart paper.

11. Ask the children what they notice that is the same about the words. Anything different?

12. Show the children that the only difference in each -at word is the beginning sound. The middle and ending sounds are the same.

13. Ask the children for other words in the -at word family.

14. Show the children the -at blending strip and hat. Say "at" out loud. Tell the children you will now show them words that belong to the -at word family.

15. Move the blending strip to create all the -at word-family words. Say the words as you create them. Have the children repeat them after you. Repeat this activity several times.

16. Explain to the children they will make their own -at blending strip.

-at Blending Strip Activity

Materials

- Line master of hat
- Blending strip with letters: *b, c, f, h, m, N, p, r, s, v, ch, dr, fl, th* (You may edit the letters on the strip.)
- Blank writing paper
- Line master of -at word family flashcards
- Crayons
- Scissors

Procedure

1. Give children the line master of the hat, scissors, and crayons.
2. Children color in the hat.
3. Children cut out the hat.
4. Cut two 1-inch vertical slits to the left of the chunk printed on the blending strip. Be sure to leave a 1-inch space between the slits.
5. Slide the strip through the slits.
6. Children read all the -at words to you by sliding the strip through the hat.
7. Vary the activity by having children read to a partner, you, or any other adult.
8. Children then write all the words on the writing paper provided.
9. Send the blending strip and flashcards home to reinforce the -at word family.

Challenge Activity

Children will turn the writing paper over and use each *-at* word in a sentence. They can also make up a silly poem of their own using some or all of the *-at* words.

Reinforcement Activity

1. For a small group mini-lesson, put the magnetic letters **c a t** on an overhead projector (or on the floor facing the children if you do not have an overhead).

2. Tell children they know the word *cat*.

3. Run your finger under the word *cat* and say *c-a-t*, stretching out the word as you say it. Again, slide your finger under the word *cat* and stretch it out. Have children say it with you this time.

4. Remove the "c" from the word and tell children this chunk of the word is *at*.

5. Put an "m" in front of the *-at* on the overhead. Again, slide your finger under the word, stretching out *m-a-t* as you say it. Repeat this procedure with the letters *b, f, h, N, p, r, s, v, ch, dr, fl, th.*

6. Have the children practice making *-at* family words individually or with a partner using the magnetic letters as you demonstrated on the overhead projector.

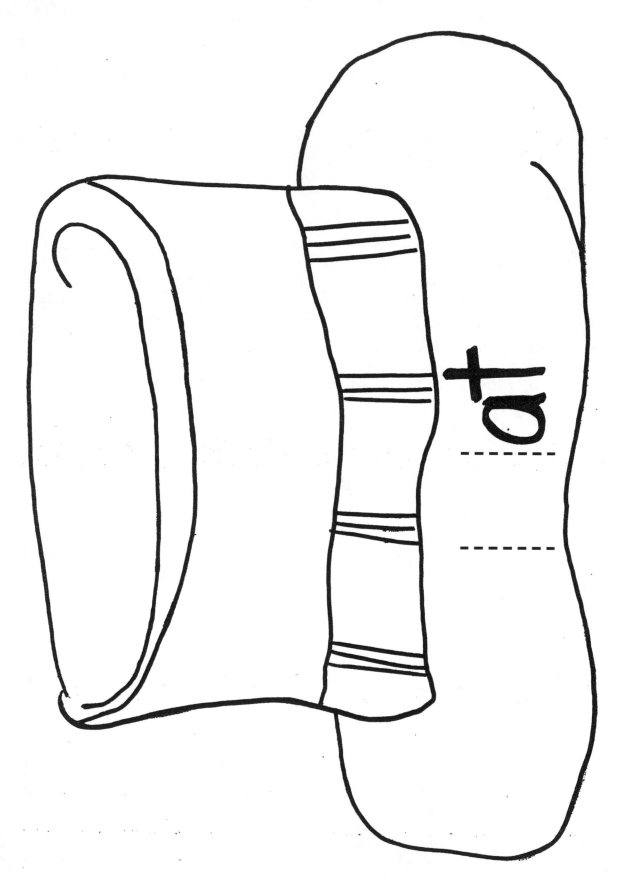

LINE MASTER—HAT BLENDING STRIP

cat	sat
fat	hat
mat	rat
bat	that

Lesson 3

Objective

- Child will read -at words in the context of a story.

Materials

- Big Book *Pat the Fat Cat*
- Little Book *Pat the Fat Cat*
- Crayons

Procedure

1. Introduce the Big Book *Pat the Fat Cat*. Read the title to the children.

2. Remind the children they have been learning about the -at word family. Elicit words from the -at word family before you begin.

3. Take a picture walk through the book. Label all the pictures. Tell the children what is happening using some of the text from the book.

4. Read the book to the children, modeling 1:1, directionality, and return sweep.

5. Reread the book, inviting the children to read along with you. Do this several times. You can vary the activity by echo reading or choral reading.

6. Give the children their own copy of the book. Have them read the book to themselves and then color in all the pictures. Have them read the book to a partner.

7. Listen to the children read the book independently or send the books home as a "read together," depending on the reading ability of each child.

Pat the Fat Cat

Name _____

Pat the fat cat got a brand new hat.

LINE MASTER—"PAT THE FAT CAT" LITTLE BOOK

"Wow!" He liked how he looked in his new hat.

"Hey, Nat!" said Pat the fat cat.
"Do you like my new hat?"

"I **like** that hat!" said Nat the rat. "Can I try it?"

- -

"Sit on the mat and try my new hat."

Nat sat on the mat and tried the hat . . .

"Oh, drat!"

LINE MASTER—"PAT THE FAT CAT" BIG BOOK

LINE MASTER—"PAT THE FAT CAT" BIG BOOK

LINE MASTER—"PAT THE FAT CAT" BIG BOOK

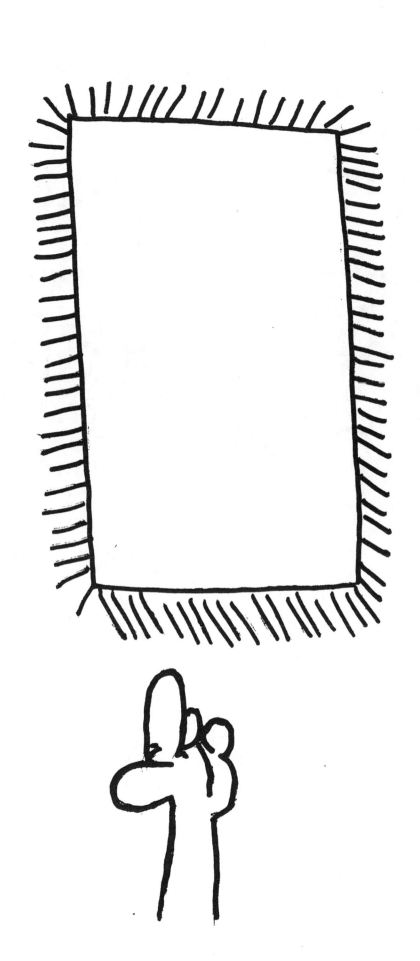

LINE MASTER—"PAT THE FAT CAT" BIG BOOK

LINE MASTER—"PAT THE FAT CAT" BIG BOOK

LINE MASTER—"PAT THE FAT CAT" BIG BOOK

Word Family

-ay

Lesson 1

Objectives

- To provide exposure and an introduction to the -*ay* word family
- To introduce the anchor word *day*

Materials

- Chart-sized poem "What Kind of Day?"
- Chart paper
- Water-based marker

Procedure

1. Brainstorm with the children all the different types of weather. This will activate prior knowledge and fill in gaps for children. List all responses on a piece of chart paper or chalkboard. You can also use a graphic organizer, such as the web shown here.

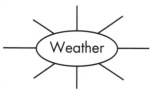

2. Tell the children you will now read a poem titled "What Kind of Day?" Read "What Kind of Day?" to the children. Model 1:1 by pointing to each word as you read. Invite the children to read through the poem with you the second time.

What Kind of Day?

What kind of day is it today?
Is it cloudy?
Is it gray?
Is it foggy?
Is it snowy?
Is it windy, gusty, blowy?
All kinds of weather make up a day.
What's the weather where you are today?

3. Vary this activity by echo reading ("My turn, your turn") and choral reading.
4. Ask the children if they can find the word *day* in the poem. Invite children to come up and circle the word *day* with a water-based marker.
5. Now do the art activity with the children, either as a small group or whole class.

Art Activity

Materials

- Pencils
- Line master of poem "What Kind of Day?"
- Line master of the weather picture
- 12" × 18" yellow construction paper
- 9-inch white paper plate
- 1-inch brass fasteners
- Crayons
- Stapler
- Black marker

Preparation

1. Reproduce the poem "What Kind of Day?" and staple it to the right side of the yellow construction paper.
2. Cut away a quarter of the paper plate.
3. Using a black marker, write the words "What Kind of Day?" on the paper plate.

Procedure

1. Children color the weather picture.
2. Staple the paper with the weather picture to the left side of the poem.
3. Children place the paper plate centered on top of the weather picture.
4. With your guidance, children push the brass fastener through the paper plate, the weather picture, and the yellow construction paper.
5. Send the poem and art activity home. This gives family members an opportunity to read the poem with the child.

Conclusion of Lesson

Bring children back to the large "What Kind of Day?" poem. Reread the poem together as a class.

What Kind of Day?

What kind of day is it today?
Is it cloudy?
Is it gray?
Is it foggy?
Is it snowy?
Is it windy, gusty, blowy?
All kinds of weather make up a day.
What's the weather where you are today?

What Kind of Day?

What kind of day is it today?
Is it cloudy?
Is it gray?
Is it foggy?
Is it snowy?
Is it windy, gusty, blowy?
All kinds of weather make up a day.
What's the weather where you are today?

LINE MASTER—WEATHER PICTURE

Lesson 2

Objectives

- Child will recognize -ay words visually and auditorily.
- Child will read words that belong in the -ay word family.

Materials

- Large copy of poem "Play All Day"
- Teacher-made model of the -ay blending strip
- Water-based marker

Procedure

1. Show children the poem "Play All Day."

Play All Day

Two little mice were playing in the hay.
"Come on!" said their mother. "You can't stay all day.
The gray cat's coming. You've got to get away!"
"Oh, please, can't we stay? Isn't there a way?"
"Let me think," said their mother.
"Hmm . . . what's today? Oh, yes! Today is Sunday.
That's the day the farmer goes away.
The gray cat's with him down by the bay."
"Hoo-ray!" said the mice. "We **can** stay and play!"
And they played in the hay all the livelong day.

---

2. Tell the children they are going to hear a poem about two little mice who like to play.
3. Read the poem to the children.
4. Ask children what they notice about the poem.
5. Read the poem again. This time emphasize the rhyming words.
6. Remind the children that words that sound alike at the end are called rhyming words.
7. Read the poem again and have the children listen for the words that rhyme. Have the children give you a "thumbs up" (or some other "secret signal") when they hear a rhyming word.
8. Circle with the water-based marker each rhyming word as it is read.
9. Read all the circled words aloud.

10. Write the circled rhyming words from the poem in a column on a separate piece of chart paper.

11. Ask the children what they notice that is the same about the words. Anything different?

12. Show the children that the only difference in each *-ay* word is the beginning sound. The middle and ending sounds are the same.

13. Ask the children for other words in the *-ay* word family.

14. Show the children the *-ay* blending strip and hay. Say "ay" out loud. Tell the children you will now show them words that belong to the *-ay* word family.

15. Move the blending strip to create all the *-ay* word-family words. Say the words as you create them. Have the children repeat them after you. Repeat this activity several times.

16. Explain to the children they will make their own *-ay* blending strip.

-ay Blending Strip Activity

Materials

- Line master of hay
- Blending strip with letters: *w, d, s, h, b, l, m, r, spr, tr, sw, pr, pl, cl, str, gr* (You may edit the letters on the strip.)
- Blank writing paper
- Line master of *-ay* word family flashcards
- Crayons
- Scissors

Procedure

1. Give children the line master of the hay, scissors, and crayons.
2. Children color in the hay.
3. Children cut out the hay.
4. Cut two 1-inch vertical slits to the left of the chunk printed on the blending strip. Be sure to leave a 1-inch space between the slits.
5. Slide the strip through the slits.
6. Children read all the *-ay* words to you by sliding the strip through the hay.
7. Vary the activity by having children read to a partner, you, or any other adult.
8. Children then write all the words on the writing paper provided.
9. Send the blending strip and flashcards home to reinforce the *-ay* word family.

Challenge Activity

Children will turn the writing paper over and use the *-ay* word in a sentence. They can also make up a silly poem of their own using some or all of the *-ay* words.

Reinforcement Activity

1. For a small group mini-lesson, put the magnetic letters **d a y** on an overhead projector (or on the floor facing the children if you do not have an overhead).

2. Tell children they know the word *day*.

3. Run your finger under the word *day* and say *d-a-y*, stretching out the word as you say it. Again, slide your finger under the word *day* and stretch it out. Have children say it with you this time.

4. Remove the "d" from the word and tell children this chunk of the word is *ay*.

5. Put an "h" in front of the *-ay* on the overhead. Again, slide your finger under the word, stretching out *h-a-y* as you say it. Repeat this procedure with the letters *w, s, b, m, l, r, spr, tr, pr, sw, pl, cl, str, gr*. Have the children practice making *-ay* family words individually or with a partner using the magnetic letters as you demonstrated on the overhead projector.

ay

LINE MASTER—HAY BLENDING STRIP

way	say
play	hay
may	day
bay	lay

LINE MASTER—AY WORD FAMILY FLASHCARDS

Lesson 3

Objective

- Child will read *-ay* words in the context of a story.

Materials

- Big Book *Play All Day*
- Little Book *Play All Day*
- Crayons

Procedure

1. Introduce the Big Book *Play All Day*. Read the title to the children.
2. Remind the children they have been learning about the *-ay* word family. Elicit words from the *-ay* word family before you begin.
3. Take a picture walk through the book. Label all the pictures. Tell the children what is happening using some of the text from the book.
4. Read the book to the children, modeling 1:1, directionality, and return sweep.
5. Reread the book, inviting the children to read along with you. Do this several times. You can vary the activity by echo reading or choral reading.
6. Give the children their own copy of the book. Have them read the book to themselves and then color in all the pictures. Have them read the book to a partner.
7. Listen to the children read the book independently or send the books home as a "read together," depending on the reading ability of each child.

Play All Day

Name _____

- -

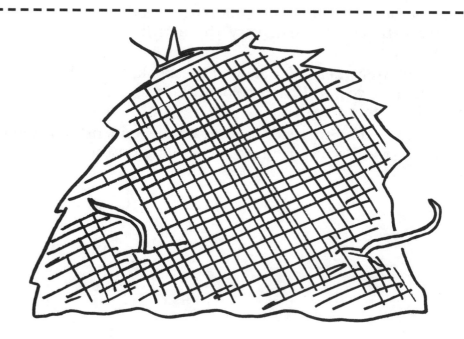

Two little mice were playing in the hay.

"Come on!" said their mother.
"You can't stay all day.
The gray cat's coming. You've got to get away!"

- -

"Oh, please, can't we stay? Isn't there a way?"

LINE MASTER—"PLAY ALL DAY" LITTLE BOOK

"Let me think," said their mother.

- -

"Hmm . . . what's today? Oh, yes! Today is
Sunday. That's the day the farmer goes away.
The gray cat's with him down by the bay."

"Hoo-ray!" said the mice. "We **can** stay
and play!"

- -

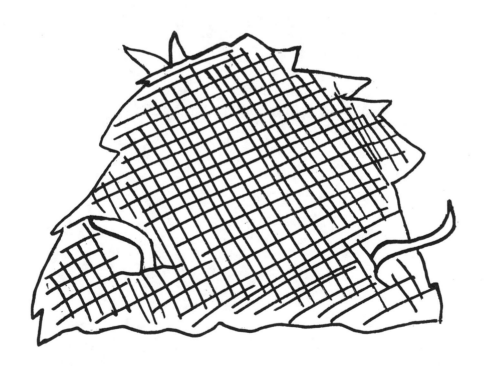

And they played in the hay all the livelong day.

LINE MASTER—"PLAY ALL DAY" LITTLE BOOK

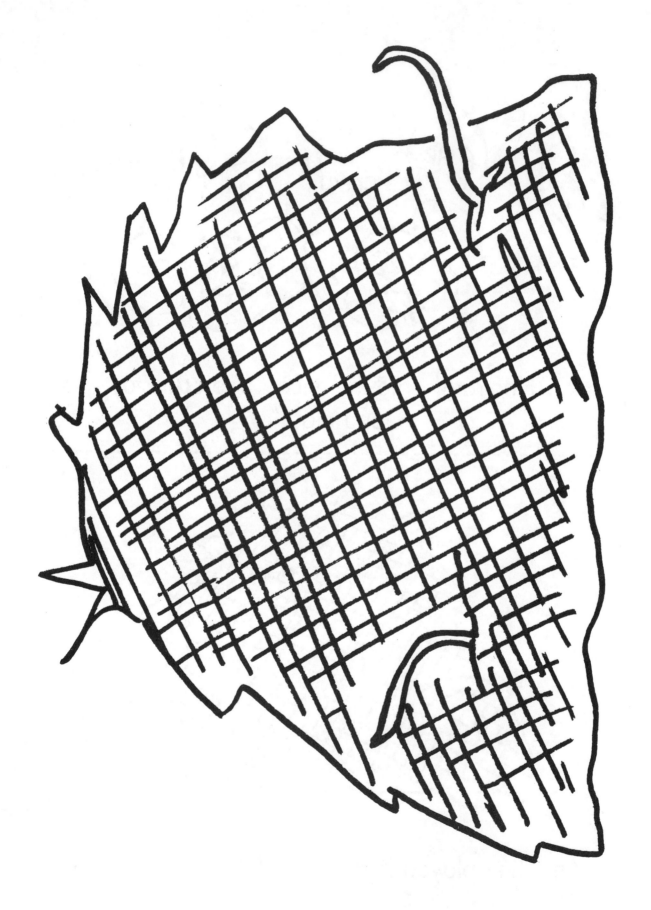

LINE MASTER—"PLAY ALL DAY" BIG BOOK

LINE MASTER—"PLAY ALL DAY" BIG BOOK

LINE MASTER—"PLAY ALL DAY" BIG BOOK

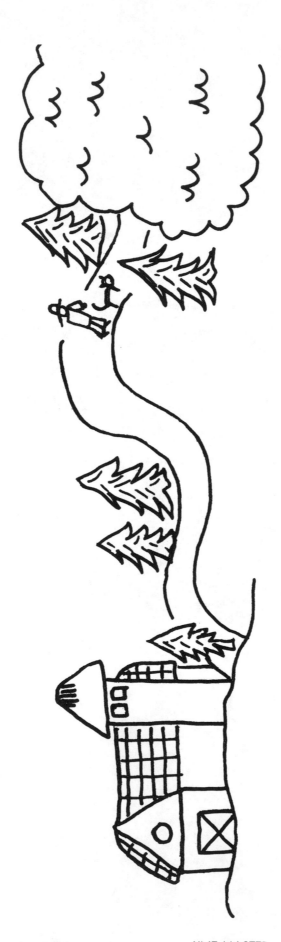

LINE MASTER—"PLAY ALL DAY" BIG BOOK

LINE MASTER—"PLAY ALL DAY" BIG BOOK

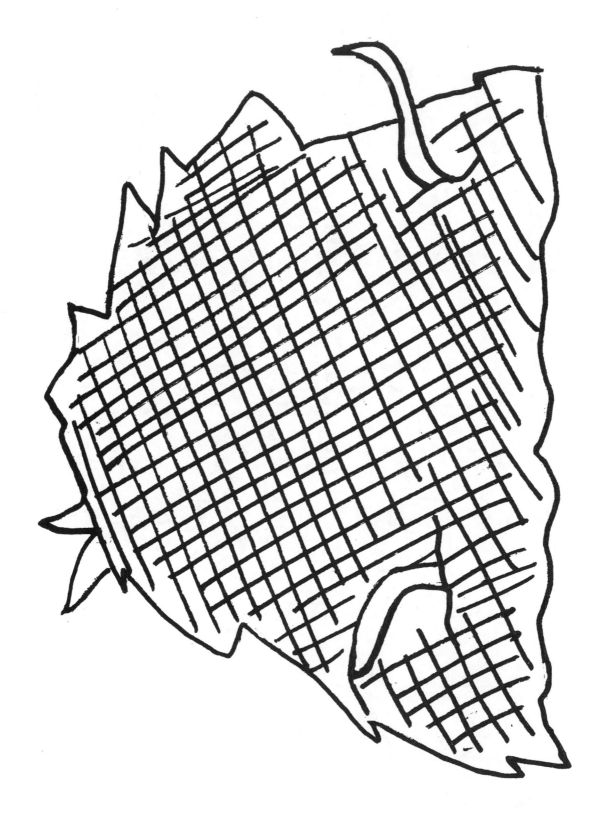

LINE MASTER—"PLAY ALL DAY" BIG BOOK

Word Family

-ed

Lesson 1

Objectives

- To provide exposure and an introduction to the -ed word family
- To introduce the anchor word bed

Materials

- Chart-sized poem "My Cozy Bed"
- Chart paper
- Water-based marker

Procedure

1. Read and discuss the book *A Bad Case of Stripes* by David Shannon. Remind the children that the girl in the story had to get back in bed when her mother discovered she was covered with stripes. Ask the children to share different times they like to be in their beds.

2. Tell the children you will now read a poem titled "My Cozy Bed." Read "My Cozy Bed" to the children. Model 1:1 by pointing to each word as you read. Invite the children to read through the poem with you the second time.

> **My Cozy Bed**
>
> My cozy bed, so comfy to me,
> always ready and waiting for me.
> When I'm tired, it's always there,
> I can cuddle and snuggle without a care.
> When I just want to be by myself,
> I curl up in bed with a book from my shelf.
> My cozy bed, so comfy to me,
> I know you'll always have room for me.

3. Vary this activity by echo reading ("My turn, your turn") and choral reading.

127

4. Ask the children if they can find the word *bed* in the poem. Invite children to come up and circle the word *bed* with a water-based marker.

5. Now do the art activity with the children, either as a small group or whole class.

Art Activity

Materials

- Line master of poem "My Cozy Bed"
- Line master of bed
- 12" × 18" purple construction paper
- Stapler
- Crayons

Preparation

Reproduce the poem "My Cozy Bed." Hold the purple construction paper vertically and staple the poem to the top of the purple construction paper.

Procedure

1. Children color in the bed and quilt.
2. Staple the bed and quilt onto the purple paper.
3. Send the poem and art activity home. This gives family members an opportunity to read the poem with the child.

Conclusion of Lesson

Bring children back to the large "My Cozy Bed" poem. Reread the poem together as a class.

My Cozy Bed

My cozy bed, so comfy to me,
always ready and waiting for me.
When I'm tired, it's always there,
I can cuddle and snuggle without a care.
When I just want to be by myself,
I curl up in bed with a book from my shelf.
My cozy bed, so comfy to me,
I know you'll always have room for me.

My Cozy Bed

My cozy bed, so comfy to me,
always ready and waiting for me.
When I'm tired, it's always there,
I can cuddle and snuggle without a care.
When I just want to be by myself,
I curl up in bed with a book from my shelf.
My cozy bed, so comfy to me,
I know you'll always have room for me.

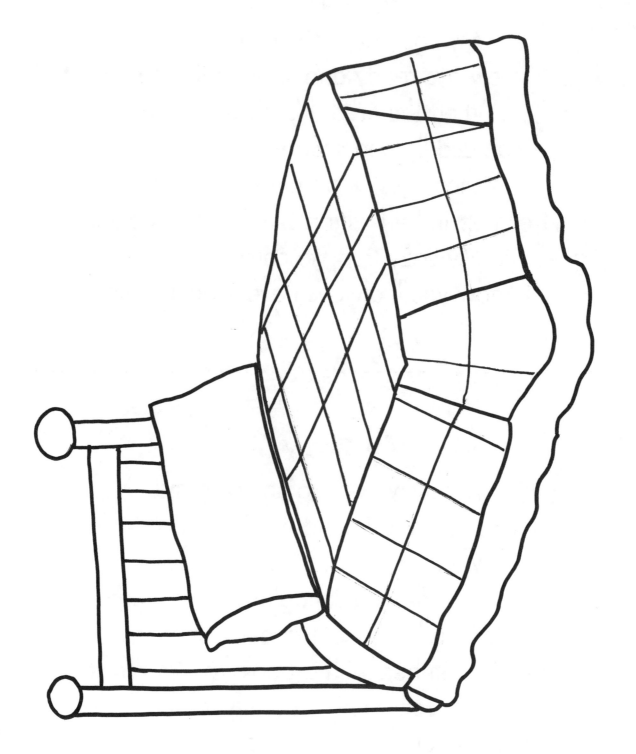

LINE MASTER—BED

Lesson 2

Objectives

- Child will recognize *-ed* words visually and auditorily.
- Child will read words that belong in the *-ed* word family.

Materials

- Large copy of poem "My Red Sled"
- Teacher-made model of the *-ed* blending strip
- Water-based marker

Procedure

1. Show children the poem "My Red Sled."

> **My Red Sled**
>
> I love to ride on my red sled.
> I keep it tucked away in the shed.
> My red sled led me down the hill.
> My red sled led me through the snow so still.
> My red sled led me around the trees.
> With the wind in my face,
> I can feel the breeze.
> My red sled I love to ride.
> Over the snow we slip and slide!

2. Tell the children they are going to hear a poem about a child who has a red sled.
3. Ask children what they notice about the poem.
4. Read the poem to the children.
5. Read the poem again. This time emphasize the rhyming words.
6. Remind the children that words that sound alike at the end are called rhyming words.
7. Read the poem again and have the children listen for the words that rhyme. Have the children give you a "thumbs up" (or some other "secret signal") when they hear a rhyming word.
8. Circle with the water-based marker each rhyming word as it is read.
9. Read all the circled words aloud.
10. Write the circled rhyming words from the poem in a column on a separate piece of chart paper.

11. Ask the children what they notice that is the same about the words. Anything different?

12. Show the children that the only difference in each *-ed* word is the beginning sound. The middle and ending sounds are the same.

13. Ask the children for other words in the *-ed* word family.

14. Show the children the *-ed* blending strip and red crayon. Say "ed" out loud. Tell the children you will now show them words that belong to the *-ed* word family.

15. Move the blending strip to create all the *-ed* word-family words. Say the words as you create them. Have the children repeat them after you. Repeat this activity several times.

16. Explain to the children they will make their own *-ed* blending strip.

-ed Blending Strip Activity

Materials

- Line master of red crayon
- Blending strip with letters: *b, f, l, w, r, T, sl, sh* (You may edit the letters on the strip.)
- Blank writing paper
- Line master of *-ed* word family flashcards
- Crayons
- Scissors

Procedure

1. Give children the line master of the red crayon, scissors, and crayons.

2. Children color in the red crayon.

3. Children cut out the red crayon.

4. You cut two 1-inch vertical slits to the left of the chunk printed on the blending strip. Be sure to leave a 1-inch space between the slits.

5. Slide the strip through the slits.

6. Children read all the *-ed* words to you by sliding the strip through the red crayon.

7. Vary the activity by having children read to a partner, you, or any other adult.

8. Children then write all the words on the writing paper provided.

9. Send the blending strip and flashcards home to reinforce the *-ed* word family.

Challenge Activity

Children will turn the writing paper over and use each of the *-ed* words in a sentence. They can also make up a silly poem of their own using some or all of the *-ed* words.

Reinforcement Activity

1. For a small group mini-lesson, put the magnetic letters **r e d** on an overhead projector (or on the floor facing the children if you do not have an overhead).

2. Tell children they know the word *red*.

3. Run your finger under the word *red* and say *r-e-d*, stretching out the word as you say it. Again, slide your finger under the word *red* and stretch it out. Have children say it with you this time.

4. Remove the "r" from the word and tell children this chunk of the word is *ed*.

5. Put a "b" in front of the *-ed* on the overhead. Again, slide your finger under the word, stretching out *b-e-d* as you say it. Repeat this procedure with the letters *f, l, T, w, sl, sh*. Have the children practice making *-ed* family words individually or with a partner using the magnetic letters as you demonstrated on the overhead projector.

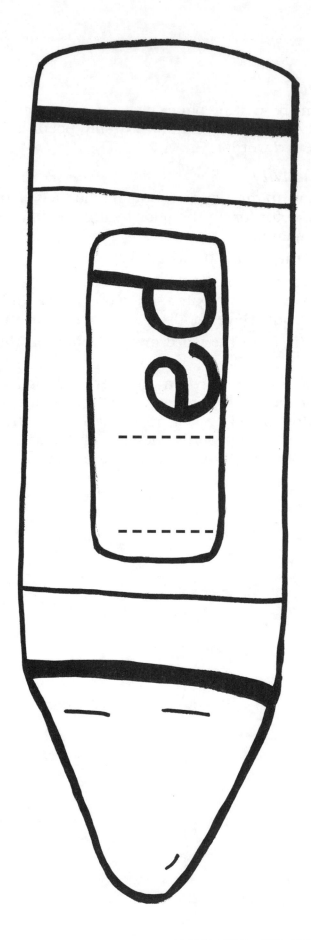

LINE MASTER—RED CRAYON BLENDING STRIP

bed	red
fed	Ted
led	sled
wed	shed

Lesson 3

Objective

- Child will read *-ed* words in the context of a story.

Materials

- Big Book *My Red Sled*
- Little Book *My Red Sled*
- Crayons

Procedure

1. Introduce the Big Book *My Red Sled.* Read the title to the children.

2. Remind the children they have been learning about the *-ed* word family. Elicit words from the *-ed* word family before you begin.

3. Take a picture walk through the book. Label all the pictures. Tell the children what is happening using some of the text from the book.

4. Read the book to the children, modeling 1:1, directionality, and return sweep.

5. Reread the book, inviting the children to read along with you. Do this several times. You can vary the activity by echo reading or choral reading.

6. Give the children their own copy of the book. Have them read the book to themselves and then color in all the pictures. Have them read the book to a partner.

7. Listen to the children read the book independently or send the books home as a "read together," depending on the reading ability of each child.

My Red Sled

Name _____

- -

I love to ride on my red sled.

I keep it tucked away in the shed.

- -

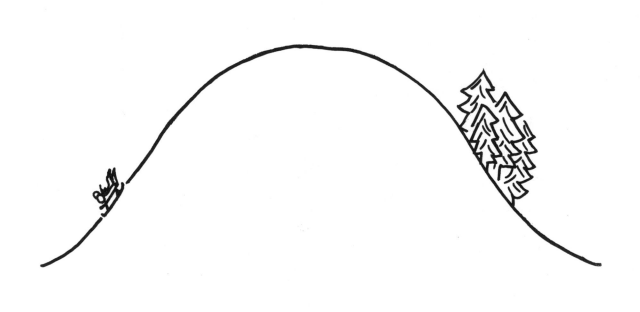

My red sled led me down the hill.

LINE MASTER—"MY RED SLED" LITTLE BOOK

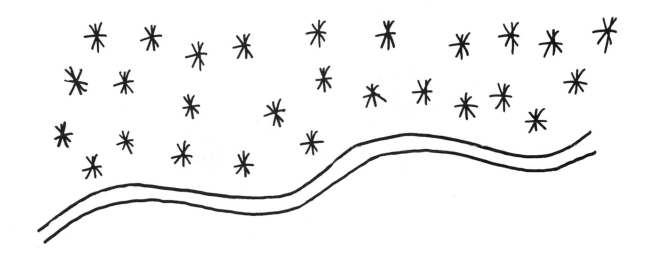

My red sled led me through the snow so still.

My red sled led me around the trees.

With the wind in my face, I can feel the breeze.

My red sled I love to ride.
Over the snow we slip and slide!

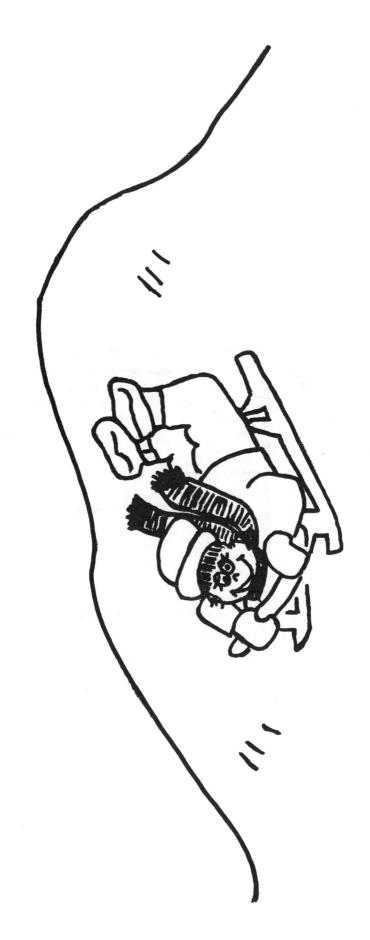

LINE MASTER—"MY RED SLED" BIG BOOK

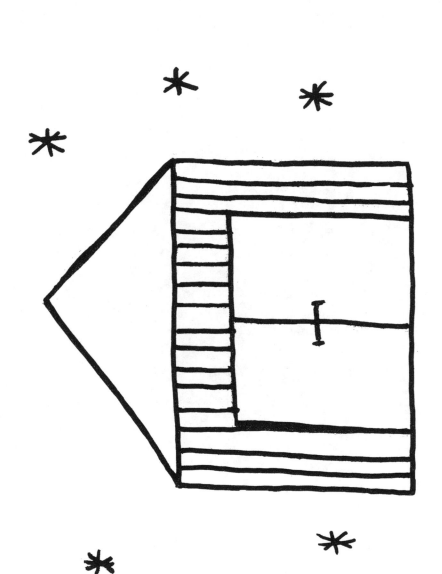

LINE MASTER—"MY RED SLED" BIG BOOK

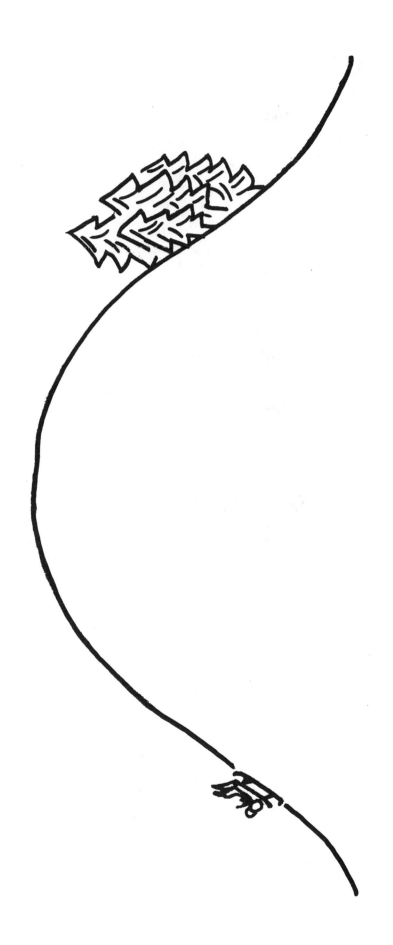

LINE MASTER—"MY RED SLED" BIG BOOK

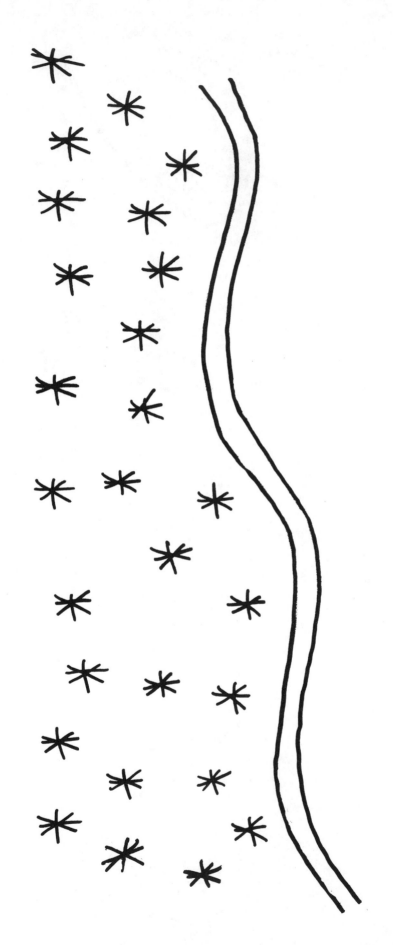

LINE MASTER—"MY RED SLED" BIG BOOK

LINE MASTER—"MY RED SLED" BIG BOOK

LINE MASTER—"MY RED SLED" BIG BOOK

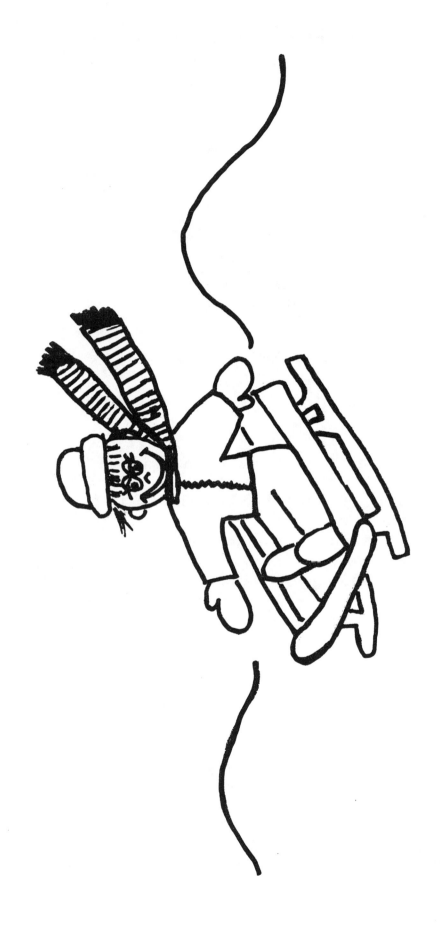

LINE MASTER—"MY RED SLED" BIG BOOK

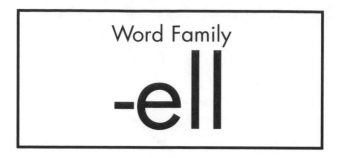

Lesson 1

Objectives

- To provide exposure and an introduction to the *-ell* word family
- To introduce the anchor word *well*

Materials

- Chart-sized poem "The Wishing Well"
- Chart paper
- Water-based marker

Procedure

1. Ask the children if they have ever made a wish. Ask them to tell how they made their wish (blowing out a candle on a birthday cake, wishing on a star, throwing a coin in a fountain, wishing on a bale of hay, etc.)

2. Tell the children people make wishes in many ways.

3. Tell the children you will now read a poem titled "The Wishing Well." Read "The Wishing Well" to the children. Model 1:1 by pointing to each word as you read. Invite the children to read through the poem with you the second time.

> **The Wishing Well**
>
> Throw a coin in the wishing well.
> Make a wish . . .
> Shh!
> Don't you tell!
> If you tell, it won't come true.
> So, keep it a secret,
> won't you?

4. Vary this activity by echo reading ("My turn, your turn") and choral reading.

5. Ask the children if they can find the word *well* in the poem. Invite children to come up and circle the word *well* with a water-based marker.

6. Now do the art activity with the children, either as a small group or whole class.

Art Activity

Materials

- Crayons
- Line master of poem "The Wishing Well"
- Line master of wishing well
- 12" × 18" red construction paper
- 4" × 4" brown construction paper squares
- Stapler
- Pencils
- Scissors
- Glue

Preparation

Reproduce the poem "The Wishing Well" and staple it to the right side of the red construction paper.

Procedure

1. Children complete the sentence: I wished for _____.
2. Children color the wishing well.
3. Children cut out small circles (coins) from the brown construction paper.
4. Children glue their coins around the wishing well.
5. Staple the wishing well to the left side of the poem
6. Send the poem and art activity home. This gives family members an opportunity to read the poem with the child.

Conclusion of Lesson

Bring children back to the large "The Wishing Well" poem. Reread the poem together as a class.

The Wishing Well

Throw a coin in the wishing well.
Make a wish . . .
Shh!
Don't you tell!
If you tell, it won't come true.
So, keep it a secret,
won't you?

The Wishing Well

Throw a coin in the wishing well.
Make a wish . . .
Shh!
Don't you tell!
If you tell, it won't come true.
So, keep it a secret,
won't you?

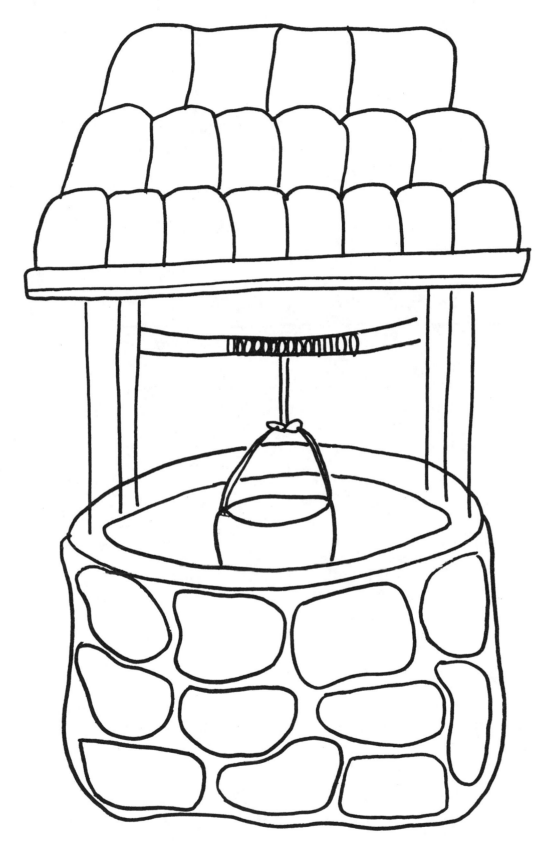

I wished for _____

LINE MASTER—WISHING WELL

Lesson 2

Objectives

- Child will recognize -*ell* words visually and auditorily.
- Child will read words that belong in the -*ell* word family.

Materials

- Large copy of poem "Show and Tell"
- Teacher-made model of the -*ell* blending strip
- Water-based marker

Procedure

1. Show children the poem "Show and Tell"

Show and Tell

One day Nell said to her friend Dell,
"Tomorrow is **my** turn for show and tell!"
"What will you bring?" asked Dell.
"It's a surprise," answered Nell.
"I'm not going to tell."
"If you won't tell . . . can I guess?" asked Dell.
"OK," said Nell. "I'll give you three tries and then I'll tell."
"Is it a shiny, silver bell?" guessed Dell.
"No, no!" said Nell. "It's not a shiny, silver bell."
"I know! Does it have a funny smell?"
"No, no!" said Nell. "It does **not** have a funny smell!"
"Is it a toy the store would sell?"
"No, no!" said Nell. "It's not a toy the store would sell.
Well . . . ," said Nell, "your three tries are over. I guess I'll have to tell.
I'm bringing my very special seashell!"
"Wow!" said Dell. "That will be a swell show and tell!"

---

2. Tell the children they are going to hear a poem about Nell and her friend Dell and what Nell is bringing for show and tell.
3. Read the poem to the children.
4. Ask children what they notice about the poem.
5. Read the poem again. This time emphasize the rhyming words.
6. Remind the children that words that sound alike at the end are called rhyming words.
7. Read the poem again and have the children listen for the words that rhyme. Have the children give you a "thumbs up" (or some other "secret signal") when they hear a rhyming word.

8. Circle with the water-based marker each rhyming word as it is read.

9. Read all the circled words aloud.

10. Write the circled rhyming words from the poem in a column on a separate piece of chart paper.

11. Ask the children what they notice that is the same about the words. Anything different?

12. Show the children that the only difference in each -ell word is the beginning sound. The middle and ending sounds are the same.

13. Ask the children for other words in the -ell word family.

14. Show the children the -ell blending strip and bell. Say "ell" out loud. Tell the children you will now show them words that belong to the -ell word family.

15. Move the blending strip to create all the -ell word-family words. Say the words as you create them. Have the children repeat them after you. Repeat this activity several times.

16. Explain to the children they will make their own -ell blending strip.

-ell Blending Strip Activity

Materials

- Line master of bell
- Blending strip with letters: *b, f, w, t, s, y, N, D, sm, sw, sh* (You may edit the letters on the strip.)
- Blank writing paper
- Line master of -ell word family flashcards
- Crayons
- Scissors

Procedure

1. Give children the line master of the bell, scissors, and crayons.

2. Children color in the bell.

3. Children cut out the bell.

4. Cut two 1-inch vertical slits to the left of the chunk printed on the blending strip. Be sure to leave a 1-inch space between the slits.

5. Slide the strip through the slits.

6. Children read all the -ell words to you by sliding the strip through the bell.

7. Vary the activity by having children read to a partner, you, or any other adult.

8. Children then write all the words on the writing paper provided.

9. Send the blending strip and flashcards home to reinforce the *-ell* word family.

Challenge Activity

Children will turn the writing paper over and use each of the *-ell* words in a sentence. They can also make up a silly poem of their own using some or all of the *-ell* words.

Reinforcement Activity

1. For a small group mini-lesson, put the magnetic letters **w e l l** on an overhead projector (or on the floor facing the children if you do not have an overhead).

2. Tell children they know the word *well*.

3. Run your finger under the word *well* and say *w-e-l-l*, stretching out the word as you say it. Again, slide your finger under the word *well* and stretch it out. Have children say it with you this time.

4. Remove the "w" from the word and tell children this chunk of the word is *ell*.

5. Put a "b" in front of the *-ell* on the overhead. Again, slide your finger under the word, stretching out *b-e-l-l* as you say it. Repeat this procedure with the letters *f, t, s, y, D, N, sm, sw, sh*.

6. Have the children practice making *-ell* family words individually or with a partner using the magnetic letters as you demonstrated on the overhead projector.

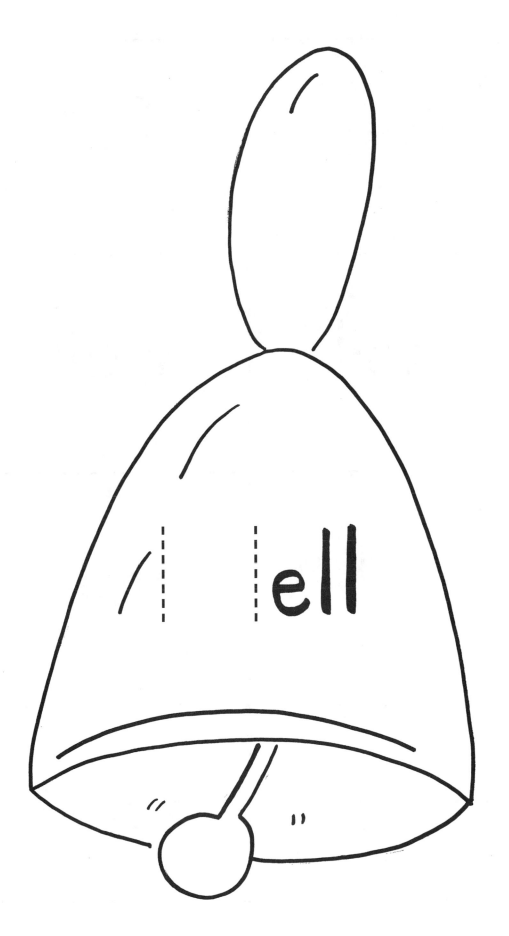

LINE MASTER—BELL BLENDING STRIP

bell	fell
sell	well
tell	yell
shell	smell

LINE MASTER—*ELL* WORD FAMILY FLASHCARDS

Lesson 3

Objective

- Child will read *-ell* words in the context of a story.

Materials

- Big Book *Show and Tell*
- Little Book *Show and Tell*
- Crayons

Procedure

1. Introduce the Big Book *Show and Tell.* Read the title to the children.
2. Remind the children they have been learning about the *-ell* word family. Elicit words from the *-ell* word family before you begin.
3. Take a picture walk through the book. Label all the pictures. Tell the children what is happening using some of the text from the book.
4. Read the book to the children, modeling 1:1, directionality, and return sweep.
5. Reread the book, inviting the children to read along with you. Do this several times. You can vary the activity by echo reading or choral reading.
6. Give the children their own copy of the book. Have them read the book to themselves and then color in all the pictures. Have them read the book to a partner.
7. Listen to the children read the book independently or send the books home as a "read together," depending on the reading ability of each child.

Show and Tell

Name _____

- -

One day Nell said to her friend Dell,
"Tomorrow is **my** turn for show and tell!"

LINE MASTER—"SHOW AND TELL" LITTLE BOOK

"What will you bring?" asked Dell. "It's a
surprise," answered Nell. "I'm not going to tell."

"If you won't tell . . . can I guess?" asked Dell.
"OK," said Nell. "I'll give you three tries
and then I'll tell."

LINE MASTER—"SHOW AND TELL" LITTLE BOOK

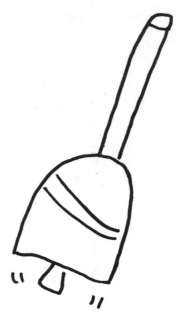

"Is it a shiny, silver bell?" guessed Dell.
"No, no!" said Nell. "It's not a shiny, silver bell."

- -

"I know! Does it have a funny smell?"
"No, no!" said Nell.
"It does **not** have a funny smell!"

"Is it a toy the store would sell?"
"No, no!" said Nell.
"It's not a toy the store would sell."

"Well . . . ," said Nell, "your three tries are over.
I guess I'll have to tell. I'm bringing my very
special seashell!" "Wow!" said Dell.
"That will be a swell show and tell!"

LINE MASTER—"SHOW AND TELL" BIG BOOK

LINE MASTER—"SHOW AND TELL" BIG BOOK

LINE MASTER—"SHOW AND TELL" BIG BOOK

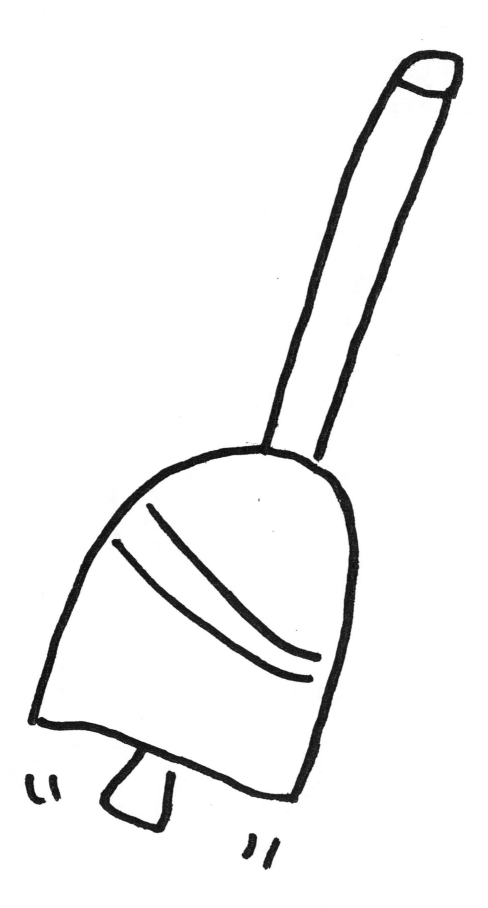

LINE MASTER—"SHOW AND TELL" BIG BOOK

LINE MASTER—"SHOW AND TELL" BIG BOOK

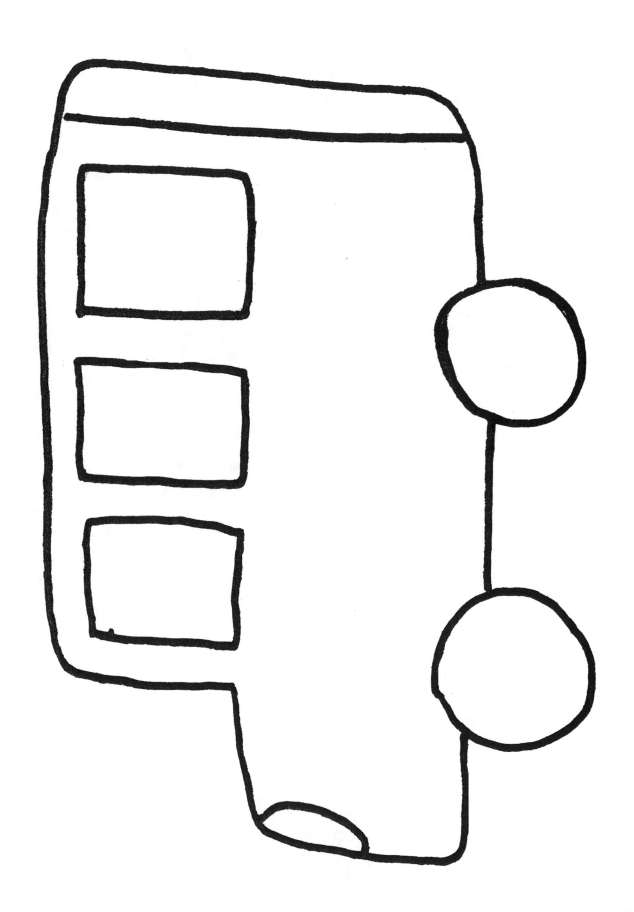

LINE MASTER—"SHOW AND TELL" BIG BOOK

LINE MASTER—"SHOW AND TELL" BIG BOOK

Word Family
-est

Lesson 1

Objectives

- To provide exposure and an introduction to the *-est* word family
- To introduce the anchor word *nest*

Materials

- Chart-sized poem "My Little Nest"
- Chart paper
- Water-based marker

Procedure

1. Read the book *The Best Nest* by P. D. Eastman.
2. Discuss the story with the children. As a group, have the children retell the story to check for comprehension.
3. Tell the children you will now read a poem titled "My Little Nest." Read "My Little Nest" to the children. Model 1:1 by pointing to each word as you read. Invite the children to read through the poem with you the second time.

> **My Little Nest**
>
> "Peep! Peep!"
> I say in my little nest.
> It's so cozy and comfy—
> My nest is best!
> I sit and watch the birds fly by
> from my little nest up in the sky.
> Here comes my mama with food for me—
> In my little nest up in the tree.

4. Vary this activity by echo reading ("My turn, your turn") and choral reading.

5. Ask the children if they can find the word *nest* in the poem. Invite children to come up and circle the word *nest* with a water-based marker.

6. Now do the art activity with the children, either as a small group or whole class.

Art Activity

Materials

- Scissors
- Crayons
- Line master of poem "My Little Nest"
- Line master of bird
- 12" × 18" blue construction paper
- 6" × 9" white construction paper
- Sponges cut into 2-inch squares
- Brown paint
- Glue
- Stapler

Preparation

Reproduce the poem "My Little Nest" and staple it to the right side of the blue construction paper.

Procedure

1. Children color the bird.
2. Children cut out the bird.
3. Children sponge-paint a nest on the white construction paper.
4. Let dry.
5. Children glue the bird on the nest.
6. Staple the nest to the left side of the poem.
7. Send the poem and art activity home. This gives family members an opportunity to read the poem with the child.

Conclusion of Lesson

Bring children back to the large "My Little Nest" poem. Reread the poem together as a class.

My Little Nest

"Peep! Peep!"
I say in my little nest.
It's so cozy and comfy—
My nest is best!
I sit and watch the birds fly by
from my little nest up in the sky.
Here comes my mama with food for me—
In my little nest up in the tree.

My Little Nest

"Peep! Peep!"
I say in my little nest.
It's so cozy and comfy—
My nest is best!
I sit and watch the birds fly by
from my little nest up in the sky.
Here comes my mama with food for me—
In my little nest up in the tree.

LINE MASTER—BIRD

Lesson 2

Objectives

- Child will recognize -est words visually and auditorily.
- Child will read words that belong in the -est word family.

Materials

- Large copy of poem "The Wild West"
- Teacher-made model of the -est blending strip
- Water-based marker

Procedure

1. Show children the poem "The Wild West."

The Wild West

Once upon a time I put on my vest
and headed out for the wild, wild west.
I heard tell of a treasure chest
with a very special golden crest.
I also heard I must beware
of a dangerous, slithering, poisonous pest.
This pest in his nest guards the treasure chest.
To open the chest I must pass the test
. . . of sneaking past the pest in the nest
and beating the rest to the treasure chest.
With vim, vigor, and zest I did it!
I passed the test!
I got past the nest and beat the rest!
Do **you** know what was in my treasure chest?

---

2. Tell the children they are going to hear a poem about a treasure chest in the wild, wild west.
3. Read the poem to the children.
4. Ask children what they notice about the poem.
5. Read the poem again. This time emphasize the rhyming words.
6. Remind the children that words that sound alike at the end are called rhyming words.
7. Read the poem again and have the children listen for the words that rhyme. Have the children give you a "thumbs up" (or some other "secret signal") when they hear a rhyming word.

8. Circle with the water-based marker each rhyming word as it is read.

9. Read all the circled words aloud.

10. Write the circled rhyming words from the poem in a column on a separate piece of chart paper.

11. Ask the children what they notice the same about the words. Anything different?

12. Show the children that the only difference in each -est word is the beginning sound. The middle and ending sounds are the same.

13. Ask the children for other words in the -est word family.

14. Show the children the -est blending strip and vest. Say "est" out loud. Tell the children you will now show them words that belong to the -est word family.

15. Move the blending strip to create all the -est word-family words. Say the words as you create them. Have the children repeat them after you. Repeat this activity several times.

16. Explain to the children they will make their own -est blending strip.

-est Blending Strip Activity

Materials
- Line master of vest
- Blending strip with letters: *n, r, b, w, j, p, t, v, z, ch, cr* (You may edit the letters on the strip.)
- Blank writing paper
- Line master of -est word family flashcards
- Crayons
- Scissors

Procedure
1. Give children the line master of the vest, scissors, and crayons.
2. Children color in the vest.
3. Children cut out the vest.
4. You cut two 1-inch vertical slits to the left of the chunk printed on the blending strip. Be sure to leave a 1-inch space between the slits.
5. Slide the strip through the slits.
6. Children read all the -est words to you by sliding the strip through the vest.

7. Vary the activity by having children read to a partner, you, or any other adult.

8. Children then write all the words on the writing paper provided.

9. Send the blending strip and flashcards home to reinforce the -est word family.

Challenge Activity

Children will turn the writing paper over and use each -est word in a sentence. They can also make up a silly poem of their own using some or all of the -est words.

Reinforcement Activity

1. For a small group mini-lesson, put the magnetic letters **w e s t** on an overhead projector (or on the floor facing the children if you do not have an overhead).

2. Tell children they know the word *west*.

3. Run your finger under the word *west* and say *w-e-s-t*, stretching out the word as you say it. Again, slide your finger under the word *west* and stretch it out. Have children say it with you this time.

4. Remove the "w" from the word and tell children this chunk of the word is *est*.

5. Put a "v" in front of the -est on the overhead. Again, slide your finger under the word, stretching out *v-e-s-t* as you say it. Repeat this procedure with the letters *n, r, b, j, p, t, z, ch, cr.*

6. Have the children practice making -est with a partner using the magnetic letters as you demonstrated on the overhead projector.

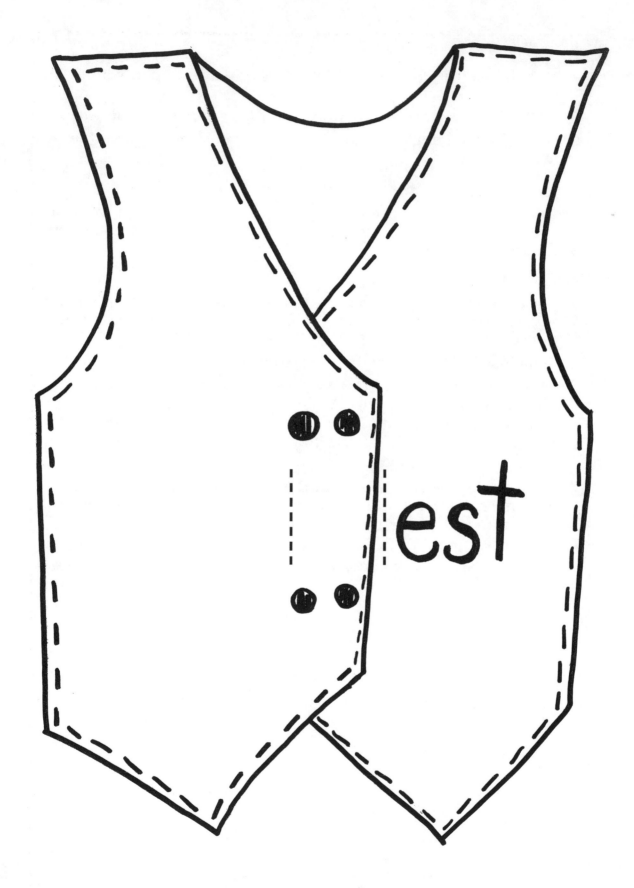

est

LINE MASTER—VEST BLENDING STRIP

nest	west
vest	best
test	rest
chest	pest

Lesson 3

Objective

- Child will read -est words in the context of a story.

Materials

- Big Book *The Wild West*
- Little Book *The Wild West*
- Crayons

Procedure

1. Introduce the Big Book *The Wild West.* Read the title to the children.

2. Remind the children they have been learning about the -est word family. Elicit words from the -est word family before you begin.

3. Take a picture walk through the book. Label all the pictures. Tell the children what is happening using some of the text from the book.

4. Read the book to the children modeling 1:1, directionality, and return sweep.

5. Reread the book, inviting the children to read along with you. Do this several times. You can vary the activity by echo reading or choral reading.

6. Give the children their own copy of the book. Have them read the book to themselves and then color in all the pictures. Have them read the book to a partner.

7. Listen to the children read the book independently or send the books home as a "read together," depending on the reading ability of each child.

The Wild West

Name _____

- -

Once upon a time I put on my vest and
headed for the wild, wild west.

I heard tell of a treasure chest
with a very special golden crest.

I also heard I must beware of a dangerous,
slithering, poisonous pest.

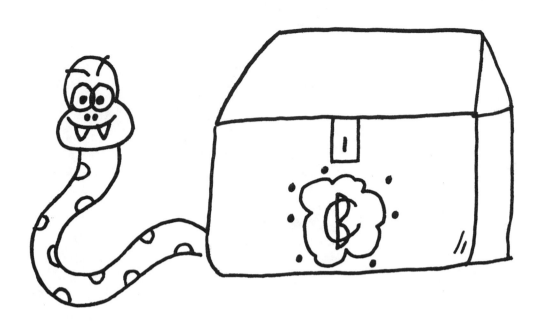

This pest in his nest guards the treasure chest.

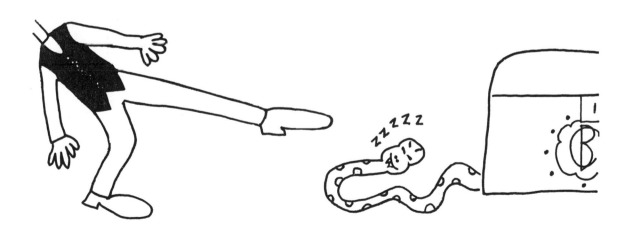

To open the chest I must pass the test . . .
of sneaking past that pest in the nest
and beating the rest to the treasure chest.

With vim, vigor, and zest I did it! I passed the test!
I got past the nest and beat the rest!

- -

Do **you** know what was in my treasure chest?

LINE MASTER—"THE WILD WEST" BIG BOOK

LINE MASTER—"THE WILD WEST" BIG BOOK

LINE MASTER—"THE WILD WEST" BIG BOOK

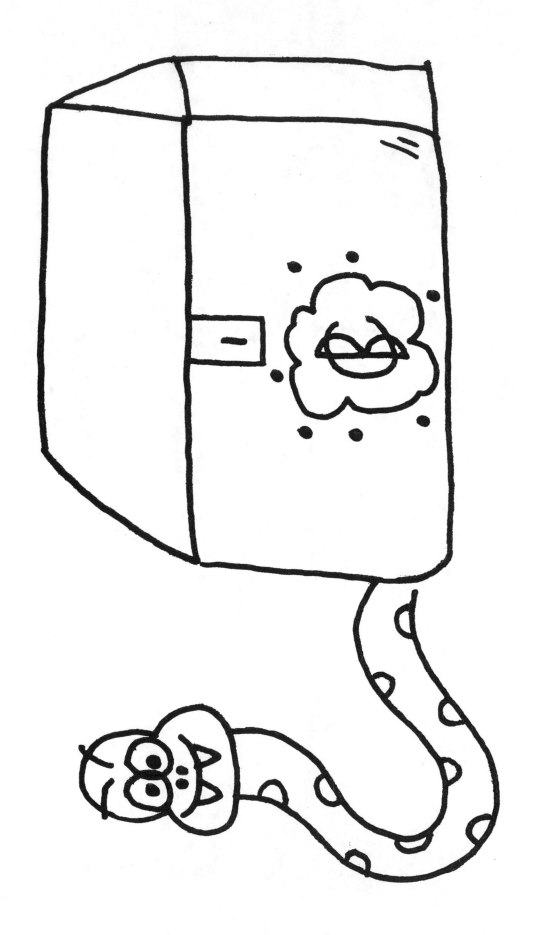

LINE MASTER—"THE WILD WEST" BIG BOOK

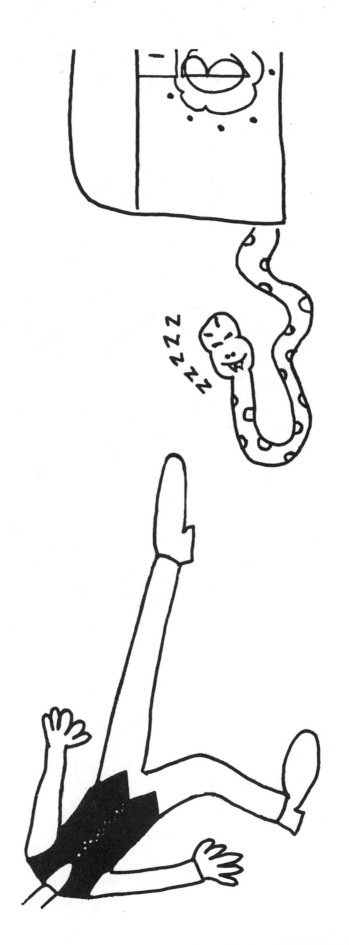

LINE MASTER—"THE WILD WEST" BIG BOOK

LINE MASTER—"THE WILD WEST" BIG BOOK

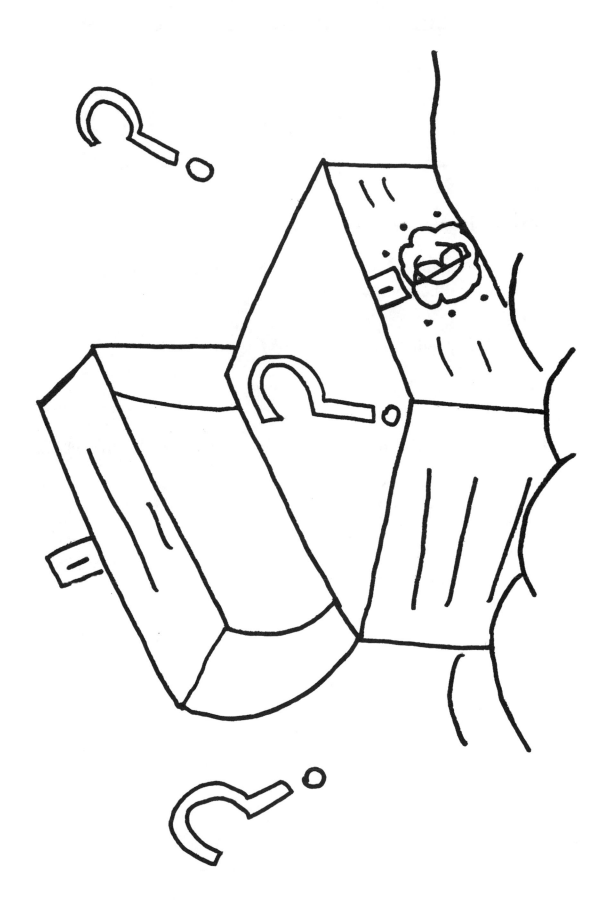

LINE MASTER—"THE WILD WEST" BIG BOOK

Word Family

-et

Lesson 1

Objectives

- To provide exposure and an introduction to the *-et* word family
- To introduce the anchor word *get*

Materials

- Chart-sized poem "Get Set"
- Chart paper
- Water-based marker

Procedure

1. Brainstorm things you can do in the snow. If you live in a climate where children are not familiar with snow, you may wish to read one of the following books before brainstorming: *Winter (Get Set . . . Go!)* by Ruth Thomson; *Snow* by Roy McKie and P. D. Eastman; *The Snowy Day* by Ezra Jack Keats.

2. Tell the children you will now read a poem titled "Get Set!" Read "Get Set!" to the children. Model 1:1 by pointing to each word as you read. Invite the children to read through the poem with you the second time.

Get Set!

On your mark,
get ready,
get set,
go!
Get your hat and mittens, too.
There's fun waiting for me and you!
We get outside.
We play in the snow.
Watch us get ready,
get set,
and go!

3. Vary this activity by echo reading ("My turn, your turn") and choral reading.

4. Ask the children if they can find the word *get* in the poem. Invite children to come up and circle the word *get* with a water-based marker.

5. Now do the art activity with the children, either as a small group or whole class.

Art Activity

Materials

- Pencils
- Markers
- Line master of poem "Get Set!"
- Line master of person
- 12" × 18" purple construction paper
- Stapler

Preparation

Reproduce the poem "Get Set!" and staple it to the right side of the purple construction paper.

Procedure

1. Children complete the sentence inside the talking bubble.
2. Children color the outline of the person in winter clothing.
3. Staple the person outline to the left side of the poem.
4. Send the poem and art activity home. This gives family members an opportunity to read the poem with the child.

Conclusion of Lesson

Bring children back to the large "Get Set!" poem. Reread the poem together as a class.

Get Set!

On your mark,
get ready,
get set,
go!
Get your hat and mittens, too.
There's fun waiting for me and you!
We get outside.
We play in the snow.
Watch us get ready,
get set,
and go!

Get Set!

On your mark,
get ready,
get set,
go!
Get your hat and mittens, too.
There's fun waiting for me and you!
We get outside.
We play in the snow.
Watch us get ready,
get set,
and go!

LINE MASTER—"GET SET!" POEM

LINE MASTER—PERSON

Lesson 2

Objectives

- Child will recognize *-et* words visually and auditorily.
- Child will read words that belong in the *-et* word family.

Materials

- Large copy of poem "The Birthday Pet"
- Teacher-made model of the *-et* blending strip
- Water-based marker

Procedure

1. Show children the poem "The Birthday Pet."

The Birthday Pet

Today's my birthday! Hip-hip-hurray!
My mom said I could get a pet.
What should I get for my birthday pet?
Should I get a pet that likes to get wet?
Or should I get a pet I can catch in a net?
Should I get a pet that isn't big yet?
I can't decide which pet to get!
Mom said, "Don't fret! I'll help you choose your birthday pet.
I know a vet who has a pet that doesn't have an owner yet!"
I was **so** happy when I met my very special birthday pet!

---

2. Tell the children they are going to hear a poem about a child who gets a very special birthday pet.
3. Read the poem to the children.
4. Ask children what they notice about the poem.
5. Read the poem again. This time emphasize the rhyming words.
6. Remind the children that words that sound alike at the end are called rhyming words.
7. Read the poem again and have the children listen for the words that rhyme. Have the children give you a "thumbs up" (or some other "secret signal") when they hear a rhyming word.
8. Circle with the water-based marker each rhyming word as it is read.
9. Read all the circled words aloud.

10. Write the circled rhyming words from the poem in a column on a separate piece of chart paper.
11. Ask the children what they notice the same about the words. Anything different?
12. Show the children that the only difference in each -et word is the beginning sound. The middle and ending sounds are the same.
13. Ask the children for other words in the -et word family.
14. Show the children the -et blending strip and jet. Say "et" out loud. Tell the children you will now show them words that belong to the -et word family.
15. Move the blending strip to create all the -et word-family words. Say the words as you create them. Have the children repeat them after you. Repeat this activity several times.
16. Explain to the children they will make their own -et blending strip.

-et Blending Strip Activity

Materials
- Line master of jet
- Blending strip with letters: *w, b, l, s, p, m, g, v, y, j, n, fr* (You may edit the letters on the strip.)
- Blank writing paper
- Line master of -et word family flashcards
- Crayons
- Scissors

Procedure
1. Give children the line master of the jet, scissors, and crayons.
2. Children color in the jet.
3. Children cut out the jet.
4. You cut two 1-inch vertical slits to the left of the chunk printed on the blending strip. Be sure to leave a 1-inch space between the slits.
5. Slide the strip through the slits.
6. Children read all the -et words to you by sliding the strip through the jet.
7. Vary the activity by having children read to a partner, you, or any other adult.
8. Children then write all the words on the writing paper provided.
9. Send the blending strip and flashcards home to reinforce the -et word family.

Challenge Activity

Children will turn the writing paper over and use each -et word in a sentence. They can also make up a silly poem of their own using some or all of the -et words.

Reinforcement Activity

1. For a small group mini-lesson, put the magnetic letters **g e t** on an overhead projector (or on the floor facing the children if you do not have an overhead).

2. Tell children they know the word get.

3. Run your finger under the word get and say g-e-t, stretching out the word as you say it. Again, slide your finger under the word get and stretch it out. Have children say it with you this time.

4. Remove the "g" from the word and tell children this chunk of the word is et.

5. Put an "l" in front of the -et on the overhead. Again, slide your finger under the word, stretching out l-e-t as you say it. Repeat this procedure with the letters w, b, s, p, m, v, y, j, n, fr.

6. Have the children practice making -et family words individually or with a partner using the magnetic letters as you demonstrated on the overhead projector.

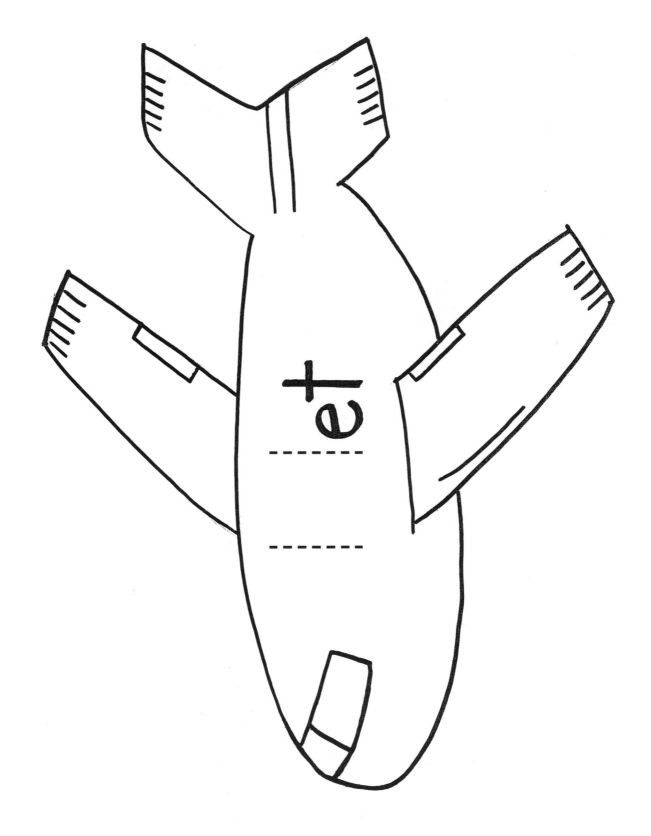

jet
- - - - - - -
- - - - - - -

LINE MASTER—JET BLENDING STRIP

get	met
pet	set
wet	bet
jet	let

Lesson 3

Objective

- Child will read *-et* words in the context of a story.

Materials

- Big Book *The Birthday Pet*
- Little Book *The Birthday Pet*
- Crayons

Procedure

1. Introduce the Big Book *The Birthday Pet*. Read the title to the children.
2. Remind the children they have been learning about the *-et* word family. Elicit words from the *-et* word family before you begin.
3. Take a picture walk through the book. Label all the pictures. Tell the children what is happening using some of the text from the book.
4. Read the book to the children, modeling 1:1, directionality, and return sweep.
5. Reread the book, inviting the children to read along with you. Do this several times. You can vary the activity by echo reading or choral reading.
6. Give the children their own copy of the book. Have them read the book to themselves and then color in all the pictures. Have them read the book to a partner.
7. Listen to the children read the book independently or send the books home as a "read together," depending on the reading ability of each child.

The Birthday Pet

Name _____

- -

Today's my birthday! Hip-hip-hurray!
My mom said I could get a pet.
What should I get for my birthday pet?

Should I get a pet that likes to get wet?

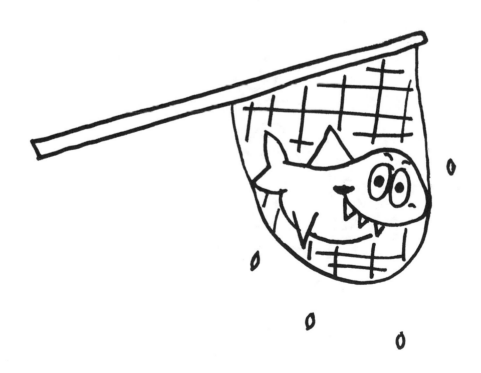

Or should I get a pet I can catch in a net?

LINE MASTER—"THE BIRTHDAY PET" LITTLE BOOK

Should I get a pet that isn't big yet?

- -

I can't decide which pet to get!

Mom said, "Don't fret! I'll help you choose your birthday pet. I know a vet who has a pet that doesn't have an owner yet!"

I was **so** happy
when I met my very special birthday pet!

LINE MASTER—"THE BIRTHDAY PET" LITTLE BOOK

LINE MASTER—"THE BIRTHDAY PET" BIG BOOK

LINE MASTER—"THE BIRTHDAY PET" BIG BOOK

LINE MASTER—"THE BIRTHDAY PET" BIG BOOK

LINE MASTER—"THE BIRTHDAY PET" BIG BOOK

LINE MASTER—"THE BIRTHDAY PET" BIG BOOK

LINE MASTER—"THE BIRTHDAY PET" BIG BOOK

Word Family

-ice

Lesson 1

Objectives

- To provide exposure and an introduction to the -ice word family
- To introduce the anchor word *dice*

Materials

- Chart-sized poem "Roll the Dice"
- Chart paper
- Water-based marker

Procedure

1. Show the children several pairs of dice. Brainstorm with the children different games they may have played using dice: Monopoly®, Yahtzee®, etc. If children have limited experiences with dice, show them how they are used.

2. Tell the children you will now read a poem titled "Roll the Dice." Read "Roll the Dice" to the children. Model 1:1 by pointing to each word as you read. Invite the children to read through the poem with you the second time.

> **Roll the Dice**
>
> Shake them up and roll away.
> Roll the dice and you can play.
> Roll the dice, first me, then you.
> You may use one or two.
> Roll them fast or roll them slow.
> Roll to see how far you go.
> Roll the dice and take your turn.
> Games with dice are fun to learn!

3. Vary this activity by echo reading ("My turn, your turn") and choral reading.

211

4. Ask the children if they can find the word *dice* in the poem. Invite children to come up and circle the word *dice* with a water-based marker.

5. Now do the art activity with the children, either as a small group or whole class.

Art Activity

Materials

- Line master of poem "Roll the Dice"
- Line master of die (This line master is to be used by *you* to create a stencil. The children will trace the stencil onto 8½" × 11" construction paper.)
- 12" × 18" black construction paper
- 8½" × 11" white construction paper (two sheets per child)
- Stapler
- Pencils
- Black markers

Preparation

Reproduce the poem "Roll the Dice" and staple it to the right side of the black construction paper.

Procedure

1. Children trace the stencil on both pieces of white paper.
2. Children cut the white paper on the lines they have just traced.
3. Children fold the white paper on the dotted lines.
4. With teacher guidance, children tape the sides of the cube to form a die.
5. Using a black marker, children carefully draw dots on each side of the cube to make a die.
6. Glue the dice onto the black paper.
7. Let dry.
8. Send the poem and art activity home. This gives family members an opportunity to read the poem with the child.

Conclusion of Lesson

Bring children back to the large "Roll the Dice" poem. Reread the poem together as a class.

Roll the Dice

Shake them up and roll away.
Roll the dice and you can play.
Roll the dice, first me, then you.
You may use one or two.
Roll them fast or roll them slow.
Roll to see how far you go.
Roll the dice and take your turn.
Games with dice are fun to learn!

Roll the Dice

Shake them up and roll away.
Roll the dice and you can play.
Roll the dice, first me, then you.
You may use one or two.
Roll them fast or roll them slow.
Roll to see how far you go.
Roll the dice and take your turn.
Games with dice are fun to learn!

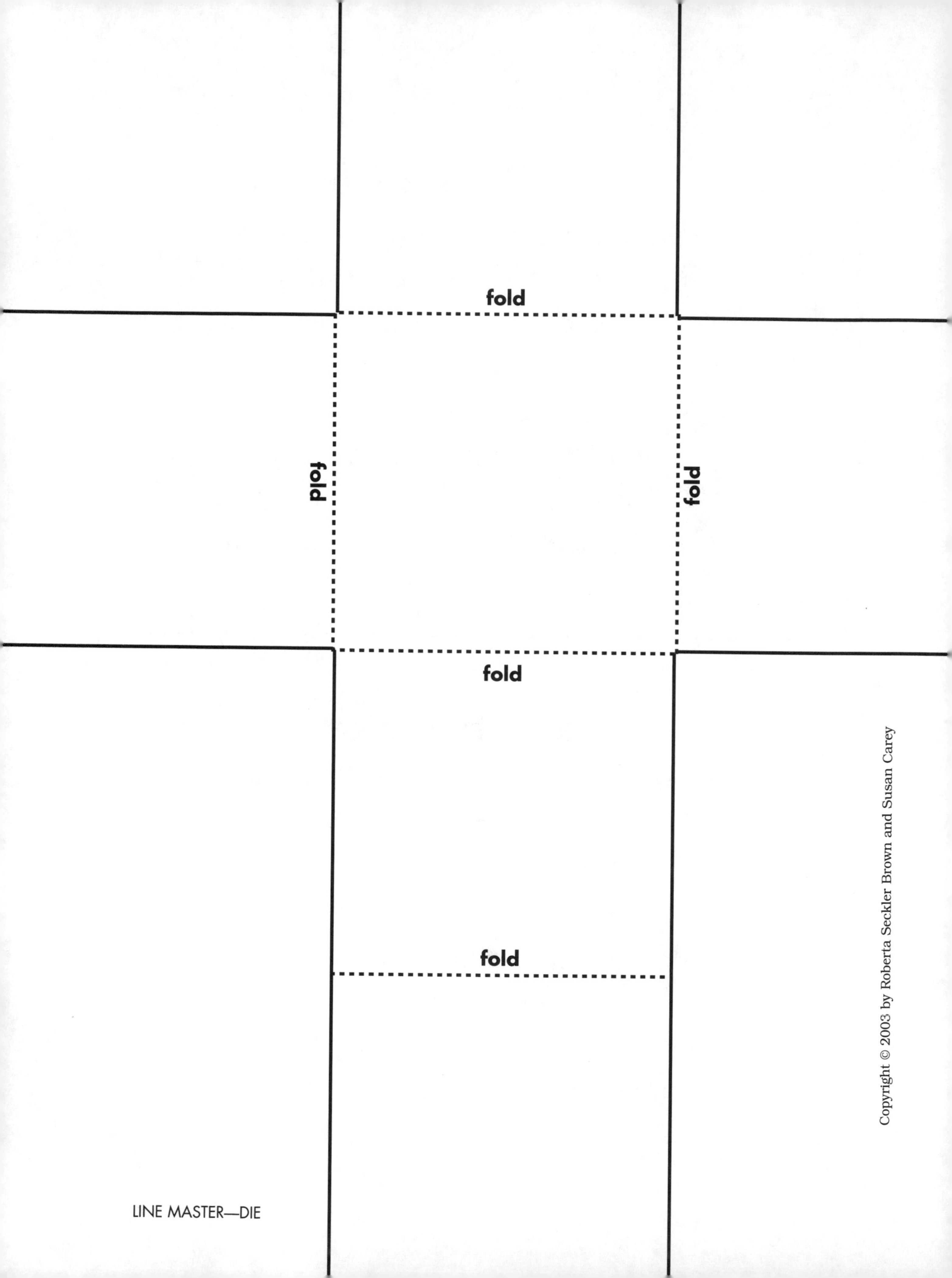

fold

fold

fold

fold

fold

LINE MASTER—DIE

Lesson 2

Objectives

- Child will recognize *-ice* words visually and auditorily.
- Child will read words that belong in the *-ice* word family.

Materials

- Large copy of poem "Twice-Cooked Rice"
- Teacher-made model of the *-ice* blending strip
- Water-based marker

Procedure

1. Show children the poem "Twice-Cooked Rice."

Twice-Cooked Rice

Once upon a time there were two mice
who liked to eat twice-cooked rice.
They sliced and diced and cooked their rice.
They did it once. They did it twice.
"This rice tastes nice!" said the mice.
"But it could use a bit of spice.
Let's ask our friends to join us.
It's always nice to share.
This rice is even better than a chocolate eclair!"

---

2. Tell the children they are going to hear a poem about two mice who cook some rice.
3. Read the poem to the children.
4. Ask children what they notice about the poem.
5. Read the poem again. This time emphasize the rhyming words.
6. Remind the children that words that sound alike at the end are called rhyming words.
7. Read the poem again and have the children listen for the words that rhyme. Have the children give you a "thumbs up" (or some other "secret signal") when they hear a rhyming word.
8. Circle with the water-based marker each rhyming word as it is read.
9. Read all the circled words aloud.
10. Write the circled rhyming words from the poem in a column on a separate piece of chart paper.

11. Ask the children what they notice that is the same about the words. Anything different?

12. Show the children that the only difference in each *-ice* word is the beginning sound. The middle and ending sounds are the same.

13. Ask the children for other words in the *-ice* word family.

14. Show the children the *-ice* blending strip and mice. Say "ice" out loud. Tell the children you will now show them words that belong to the *-ice* word family.

15. Move the blending strip to create all the *-ice* word-family words. Say the words as you create them. Have the children repeat them after you. Repeat this activity several times.

16. Explain to the children they will make their own *-ice* blending strip.

-ice Blending Strip Activity

Materials

- Line master of mice
- Blending strip with letters: *n, r, m, d, sl, pr, tw* (You may edit the letters on the strip.)
- Blank writing paper
- Line master of *-ice* word family flashcards
- Crayons
- Scissors

Procedure

1. Give children the line master of the mice, scissors, and crayons.
2. Children color in the mice.
3. Children cut out the mice.
4. Cut two 1-inch vertical slits to the left of the chunk printed on the blending strip. Be sure to leave a 1-inch space between the slits.
5. Slide the strip through the slits.
6. Children read all the *-ice* words to you by sliding the strip through the mice.
7. Vary the activity by having children read to a partner, you, or any other adult.
8. Children then write all the words on the writing paper provided.
9. Children cut the *-ice* word family flashcards on the lines provided.
10. Send the blending strip and flashcards home to reinforce the *-ice* word family.

Challenge Activity

Children will turn the writing paper over and use each -ice word in a sentence. They can also make up a silly poem of their own using some or all of the -ice words.

Reinforcement Activity

1. For a small group mini-lesson, put the magnetic letters **m i c e** on an overhead projector (or on the floor facing the children if you do not have an overhead).

2. Tell children they know the word *mice*.

3. Run your finger under the word *mice* and say *m-i-c-e*, stretching out the word as you say it. Again, slide your finger under the word *mice* and stretch it out. Have children say it with you this time.

4. Remove the "m" from the word and tell children this chunk of the word is *ice*.

5. Put an "r" in front of the -ice on the overhead. Again, slide your finger under the word, stretching out *r-i-c-e* as you say it. Repeat this procedure with the letters *d, n, pr, tw,* and *sl.* Have the children practice making -ice family words individually or with a partner using the magnetic letters as you demonstrated on the overhead projector.

ice

LINE MASTER—MICE BLENDING STRIP

nice	rice
dice	slice
price	twice

Lesson 3

Objective

- Child will read -*ice* words in the context of a story.

Materials

- Big Book *Twice-Cooked Rice*
- Little Book *Twice-Cooked Rice*
- Crayons

Procedure

1. Introduce the Big Book *Twice-Cooked Rice*. Read the title to the children.

2. Remind the children they have been learning about the -*ice* word family. Elicit words from the -*ice* word family before you begin.

3. Take a picture walk through the book. Label all the pictures. Tell the children what is happening using some of the text from the book.

4. Read the book to the children, modeling 1:1, directionality, and return sweep.

5. Reread the book, inviting the children to read along with you. Do this several times. Vary the activity by echo reading or choral reading.

6. Give the children their own copy of the book. Have them read the book to themselves and then color in all the pictures. Have them read the book to a partner.

7. Listen to the children read the book independently or send the books home as a "read together," depending on the reading ability of each child.

Twice-Cooked Rice

Name _____

- -

Once upon a time there were two mice
who liked to eat twice-cooked rice.

They sliced and diced and cooked their rice.

They did it once. They did it twice.

"This rice tastes nice!" said the mice.

"But it could use a bit of spice."

LINE MASTER—"TWICE-COOKED RICE" LITTLE BOOK

"Let's ask our friends to join us.
It's always nice to share."

"This rice is even better than a chocolate eclair!"

LINE MASTER—"TWICE-COOKED RICE" BIG BOOK

LINE MASTER—"TWICE-COOKED RICE" BIG BOOK

LINE MASTER—"TWICE-COOKED RICE" BIG BOOK

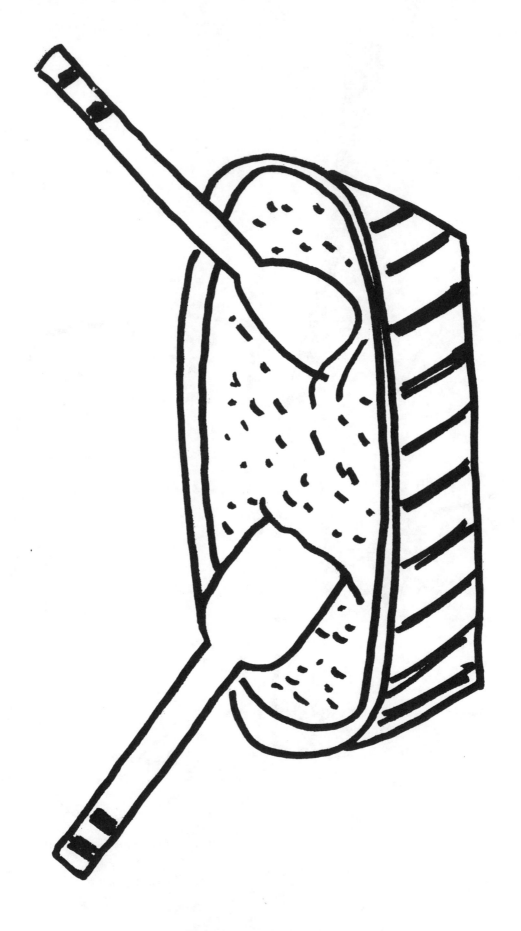

LINE MASTER—"TWICE-COOKED RICE" BIG BOOK

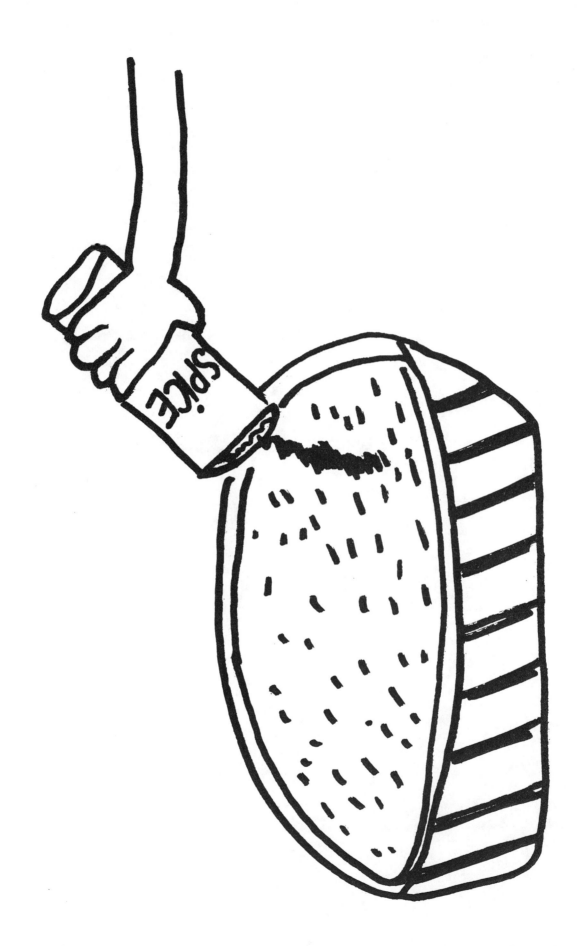

LINE MASTER—"TWICE-COOKED RICE" BIG BOOK

LINE MASTER—"TWICE-COOKED RICE" BIG BOOK

LINE MASTER—"TWICE-COOKED RICE" BIG BOOK

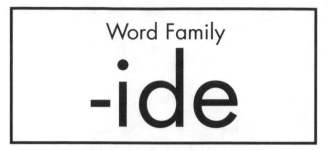

Word Family
-ide

Lesson 1

Objectives

- To provide exposure and an introduction to the -*ide* word family
- To introduce the anchor word *ride*

Materials

- Chart-sized poem "Ride Up and Away!"
- Chart paper
- Water-based marker

Procedure

1. Brainstorm with children what they would see if they were floating in the air in a hot air balloon. This will activate prior knowledge and fill in gaps for children. List all responses on a piece of chart paper or chalkboard. You can also use a graphic organizer, such as the web shown here.

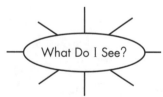

What Do I See?

2. Tell the children you will now read a poem titled "Ride Up and Away!" Read "Ride Up and Away!" to the children. Model 1:1 by pointing to each word as you read. Invite the children to read through the poem with you the second time.

Ride Up and Away!

Would you like to ride way up high?
Ride a balloon up in the sky.
Let the wind take you to and fro,
from the top of the mountain to the sea below.
Think of all the places you could go.

---

3. Vary this activity by echo reading ("My turn, your turn") and choral reading.

4. Ask the children if they can find the word *ride* in the poem. Invite children to come up and circle the word *ride* with a water-based marker.

5. Now do the art activity with the children, either as a small group or whole class.

Art Activity

Materials

- Watercolors
- Line master of poem "Ride Up and Away!"
- Line master of hot air balloon
- 12" × 18" blue construction paper
- Stapler
- Pencils
- Crayons

Preparation

Reproduce the poem "Ride Up and Away!" and staple it to the right side of the blue construction paper.

Procedure

1. Children complete the sentence: I would ride to _____.
2. Children paint the hot air balloon.
3. Let dry.
4. Children draw themselves in the basket of the balloon.
5. Staple the hot air balloon onto the blue paper.
6. Send the poem and art activity home. This gives family members an opportunity to read the poem with the child.

Conclusion of Lesson

Bring children back to the large "Ride Up and Away!" poem. Reread the poem together as a class.

Ride Up and Away!

Would you like to ride way up high?
Ride a balloon up in the sky.
Let the wind take you to and fro,
from the top of the mountain
to the sea below.
Think of all the places you could go.

Ride Up and Away!

Would you like to ride way up high?
Ride a balloon up in the sky.
Let the wind take you to and fro,
from the top of the mountain
to the sea below.
Think of all the places you could go.

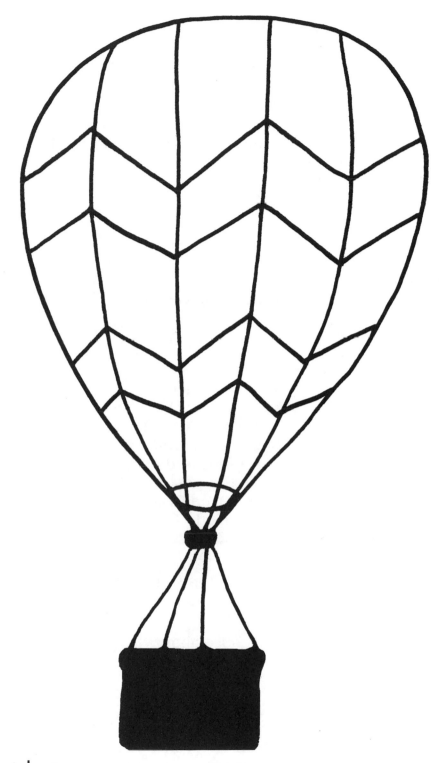

I would ride to . . .

_____

_____

_____

LINE MASTER—HOT AIR BALLOON

Lesson 2

Objectives

- Child will recognize -*ide* words visually and auditorily.
- Child will read words that belong in the -*ide* word family.

Materials

- Large copy of poem "Let's Ride"
- Teacher-made model of the -*ide* blending strip
- Water-based marker

Procedure

1. Show children the poem "Let's Ride."

Let's Ride

Get your board!
Come on, let's ride!
The waves are breaking.
Here comes the tide.
Get on that board.
Let's ride and glide.
Whee! It's fun to slip and slide.
Uh oh! A big one's coming . . .
No time to HIDE!!!

---

2. Tell the children they are going to hear a poem about a ride on a surfboard.
3. Read the poem to the children.
4. Ask children what they notice about the poem.
5. Read the poem again. This time emphasize the rhyming words.
6. Remind the children that words that sound alike at the end are called rhyming words.
7. Read the poem again and have the children listen for the words that rhyme. Have the children give you a "thumbs up" (or some other "secret signal") when they hear a rhyming word.
8. Circle with the water-based marker each rhyming word as it is read.
9. Read all the circled words aloud.
10. Write the circled rhyming words from the poem in a column on a separate piece of chart paper.

11. Ask the children what they notice that is the same about the words. Anything different?

12. Show the children that the only difference in each -*ide* word is the beginning sound. The middle and ending sounds are the same.

13. Ask the children for other words in the -*ide* word family.

14. Show the children the -*ide* blending strip and slide. Say "ide" out loud. Tell the children you will now show them words that belong to the -*ide* word family.

15. Move the blending strip to create all the -*ide* word-family words. Say the words as you create them. Have the children repeat them after you. Repeat this activity several times.

16. Explain to the children they will make their own -*ide* blending strip.

-ide Blending Strip Activity

Materials

- Line master of slide
- Blending strip with letters: *h, t, r, s, w, gl, sl* (You may edit the letters on the strip.)
- Blank writing paper
- Line master of -*ide* word family flashcards
- Crayons
- Scissors

Procedure

1. Give children the line master of the slide, scissors, and crayons.
2. Children color in the slide.
3. Children cut out the slide.
4. Cut two 1-inch vertical slits to the left of the chunk printed on the blending strip. Be sure to leave a 1-inch space between the slits.
5. Slide the strip through the slits.
6. Children read all the -*ide* words to you by sliding the strip through the slide.
7. Vary the activity by having children read to a partner, you, or any other adult.
8. Children then write all the words on the writing paper provided.
9. Send the blending strip and flashcards home to reinforce the -*ide* word family.

Challenge Activity

Children will turn the writing paper over and use each of the *-ide* words in a sentence. They can also make up a silly poem of their own using some or all of the *-ide* words.

Reinforcement Activity

1. For a small group mini-lesson, put the magnetic letters **r i d e** on an overhead projector (or on the floor facing the children if you do not have an overhead).

2. Tell children they know the word *ride*.

3. Run your finger under the word *ride* and say *r-i-d-e*, stretching out the word as you say it. Again, slide your finger under the word *ride* and stretch it out. Have children say it with you this time.

4. Remove the "r" from the word and tell children this chunk of the word is *ide*.

5. Put an "s" in front of the *-ide* on the overhead. Again, slide your finger under the word, stretching out *s-i-d-e* as you say it. Repeat this procedure with the letters *t, w, h, gl,* and *sl.* Have the children practice making *-ide* family words individually or with a partner using the magnetic letters as you demonstrated on the overhead projector.

LINE MASTER—SLIDE BLENDING STRIP

hide	tide
ride	wide
side	glide
slide	pride

Lesson 3

Objective

- Child will read -*ide* words in the context of a story.

Materials

- Big Book *Let's Ride*
- Little Book *Let's Ride*
- Crayons

Procedure

1. Introduce the Big Book *Let's Ride*. Read the title to the children.
2. Remind the children they have been learning about the -*ide* word family. Elicit words from the -*ide* word family before you begin.
3. Take a picture walk through the book. Label all the pictures. Tell the children what is happening using some of the text from the book.
4. Read the book to the children, modeling 1:1, directionality, and return sweep.
5. Reread the book, inviting the children to read along with you. Do this several times. Vary the activity by echo reading or choral reading.
6. Give the children their own copy of the book. Have them read the book to themselves and then color in all the pictures. Have them read the book to a partner.
7. Listen to the children read the book independently or send the books home as a "read together," depending on the reading ability of each child.

Let's Ride

Name _____

- -

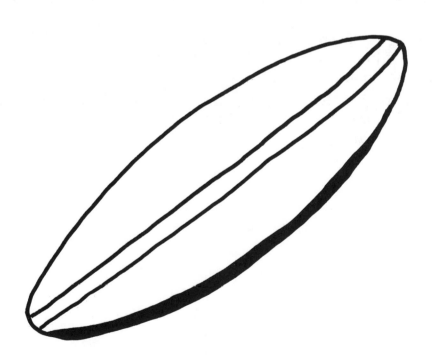

Get your board!

Come on, let's ride!

- -

The waves are breaking. Here comes the tide.

Get on that board. Let's ride and glide.

- -

Whee! It's fun to slip and slide!

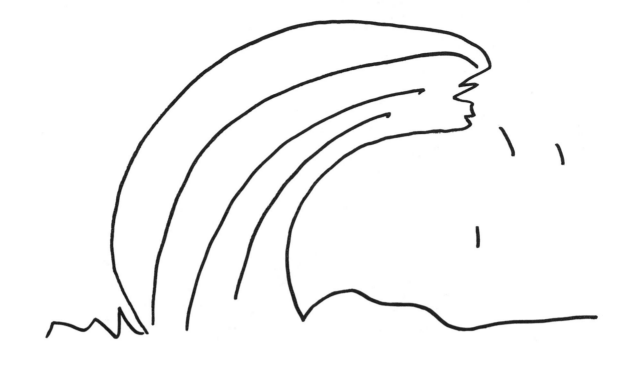

Uh oh! A big one's coming!

No time to HIDE!!!

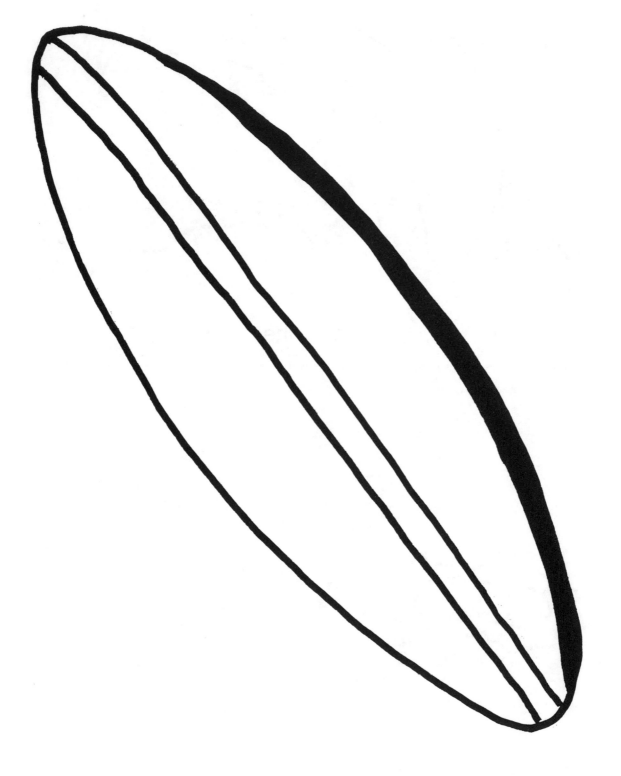

LINE MASTER—"LET'S RIDE" BIG BOOK

LINE MASTER—"LET'S RIDE" BIG BOOK

LINE MASTER—"LET'S RIDE" BIG BOOK

LINE MASTER—"LET'S RIDE" BIG BOOK

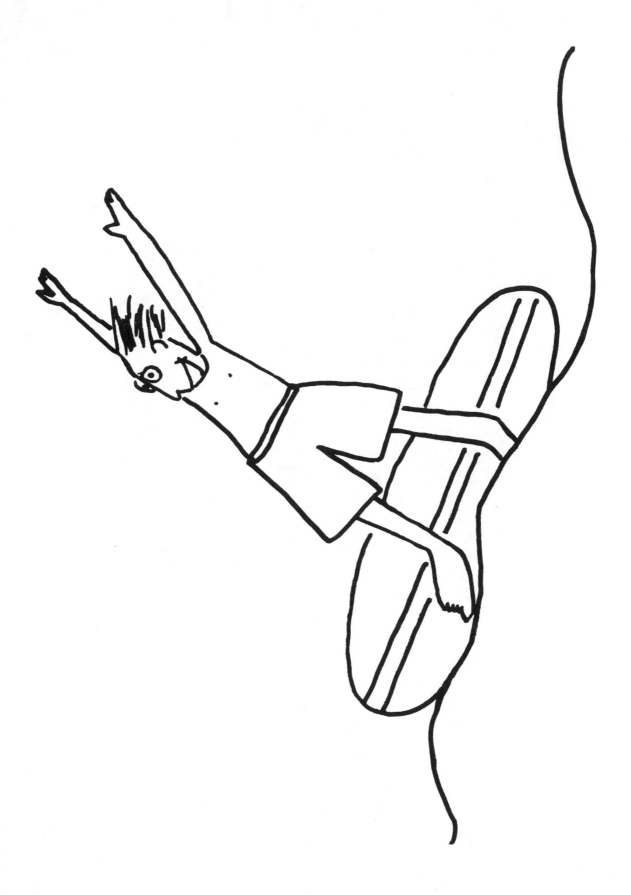

LINE MASTER—"LET'S RIDE" BIG BOOK

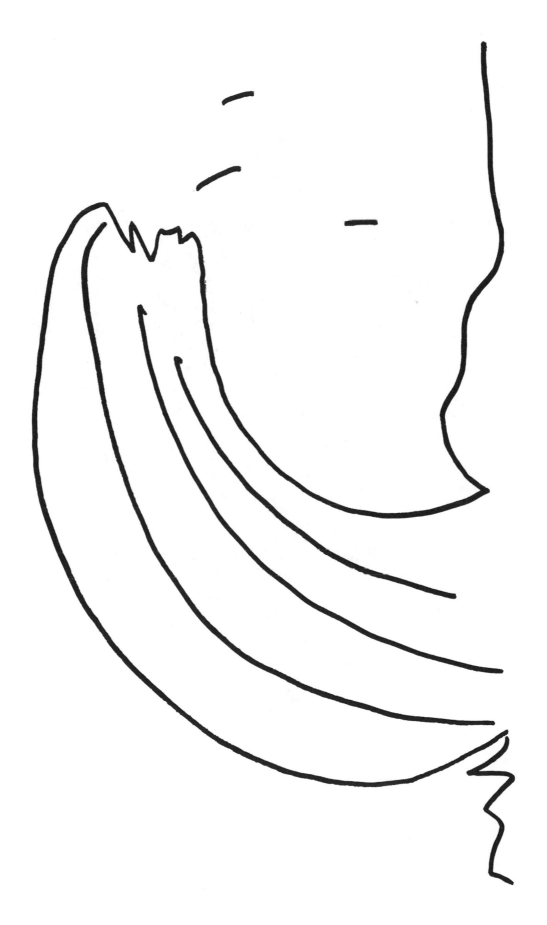

LINE MASTER—"LET'S RIDE" BIG BOOK

LINE MASTER—"LET'S RIDE" BIG BOOK

Word Family
-ig

Lesson 1

Objectives

- To provide exposure and an introduction to the -ig word family
- To introduce the anchor word wig

Materials

- Chart-sized poem "Wacky Wigs"
- Chart paper
- Water-based marker

Procedure

1. Read and discuss *Mop Top* by Don Freeman. Talk about how different hairstyles and color make a person special. However, it can be fun to temporarily change your hair by wearing a wig!

2. Tell the children you will now read a poem titled "Wacky Wigs." Read "Wacky Wigs" to the children. Model 1:1 by pointing to each word as you read. Invite the children to read through the poem with you the second time.

Wacky Wigs

A wig can be a funny way
to change the way you look today.
Some are curly.
Some are straight.
A rainbow wig is really great.
Short, long, wavy, too,
Wigs can be red, white, and blue!
So . . .
If you dare to change your hair,
a wig is what you'll have to wear!

---

3. Vary this activity by echo reading ("My turn, your turn") and choral reading.

4. Ask the children if they can find the word *wig* in the poem. Invite children to come up and circle the word *wig* with a water-based marker.

5. Now do the art activity with the children, either as a small group or whole class.

Art Activity

Materials
- Markers
- Line master of poem "Wacky Wigs"
- Line master of head
- 12" × 18" white construction paper
- Stapler
- Multicultural crayons

Preparation
Reproduce the poem "Wacky Wigs" and staple it to the right side of the white construction paper.

Procedure
1. Children color the face on the head using the multicultural crayons.
2. Children create a "wacky wig" on their head using the markers.
3. Send the poem and art activity home. This gives family members an opportunity to read the poem with the child.

Conclusion of Lesson

Bring children back to the large "Wacky Wigs" poem. Reread the poem together as a class.

Wacky Wigs

A wig can be a funny way
to change the way you look today.
Some are curly.
Some are straight.
A rainbow wig is really great.
Short, long, wavy, too,
Wigs can be red, white, and blue!
So . . .
If you dare to change your hair,
a wig is what you'll have to wear!

Wacky Wigs

A wig can be a funny way
to change the way you look today.
Some are curly.
Some are straight.
A rainbow wig is really great.
Short, long, wavy, too,
Wigs can be red, white, and blue!
So . . .
If you dare to change your hair,
a wig is what you'll have to wear!

LINE MASTER—HEAD

Lesson 2

Objectives

- Child will recognize -*ig* words visually and auditorily.
- Child will read words that belong in the -*ig* word family.

Materials

- Large copy of poem "The Big Rig"
- Teacher-made model of the -*ig* blending strip
- Water-based marker

Procedure

1. Show children the poem "The Big Rig."

> **The Big Rig**
>
> It's the day of the dig on Mr. Pig's farm.
> Here comes the big rig.
> The big rig's ready to dig, dig, dig!
> As the rig begins to dig . . .
> Mr. Pig wears a wig and does a jig.
> "Hooray for the dig!" says the pig in the wig.
> "I can roll in the mud made by the big rig."

2. Tell the children they are going to hear a poem about a big rig. Make sure the children know that a big rig is another name for a large truck.
3. Read the poem to the children.
4. Ask children what they notice about the poem.
5. Read the poem again. This time emphasize the rhyming words.
6. Remind the children that words that sound alike at the end are called rhyming words.
7. Read the poem again and have the children listen for the words that rhyme. Have the children give you a "thumbs up" (or some other "secret signal") when they hear a rhyming word.
8. Circle with the water-based marker each rhyming word as it is read.
9. Read all the circled words aloud.
10. Write the circled rhyming words from the poem in a column on a separate piece of chart paper.

11. Ask the children what they notice that is the same about the words. Anything different?

12. Show the children that the only difference in each -*ig* word is the beginning sound. The middle and ending sounds are the same.

13. Ask the children for other words in the -*ig* word family.

14. Show the children the -*ig* blending strip and pig. Say "ig" out loud. Tell the children you will now show them words that belong to the -*ig* word family.

15. Move the blending strip to create all the -*ig* word-family words. Say the words as you create them. Have the children repeat them after you. Repeat this activity several times.

16. Explain to the children they will make their own -*ig* blending strip.

-ig Blending Strip Activity

Materials
- Line master of pig
- Blending strip with letters: *p, w, j, b, f, d, r, z* (You may edit the letters on the strip.)
- Blank writing paper
- Line master of -*ig* word family flashcards
- Crayons
- Scissors

Procedure
1. Give children the line master of the pig, scissors, and crayons.
2. Children color in the pig.
3. Children cut out the pig.
4. Cut two 1-inch vertical slits to the left of the chunk printed on the blending strip. Be sure to leave a 1-inch space between the slits.
5. Slide the strip through the slits.
6. Children read all the -*ig* words to you by sliding the strip through the pig.
7. Vary the activity by having children read to a partner, you, or any other adult.
8. Children then write all the words on the writing paper provided.
9. Send the blending strip and flashcards home to reinforce the -*ig* word family.

Challenge Activity

Children will turn the writing paper over and use each of the -*ig* words in a sentence. They can also make up a silly poem of their own using some or all of the -*ig* words.

Reinforcement Activity

1. For a small group mini-lesson, put the magnetic letters **p i g** on an overhead projector (or on the floor facing the children if you do not have an overhead).
2. Tell children they know the word *pig*.
3. Run your finger under the word *pig* and say *p-i-g*, stretching out the word as you say it. Again, slide your finger under the word *pig* and stretch it out. Have children say it with you this time.
4. Remove the "p" from the word and tell children this chunk of the word is *ig*.
5. Put a "b" in front of the -*ig* on the overhead. Again, slide your finger under the word, stretching out *b-i-g* as you say it. Repeat this procedure with the letters *w, j, d, f, r,* and *z*. Have the children practice making -*ig* family words individually or with a partner using the magnetic letters as you demonstrated on the overhead projector.

LINE MASTER—PIG BLENDING STRIP

pig	wig
jig	big
fig	dig
rig	twig

LINE MASTER—*IG* WORD FAMILY FLASHCARDS

Lesson 3

Objective

- Child will read *-ig* words in the context of a story.

Materials

- Big Book *The Big Rig*
- Little Book *The Big Rig*
- Crayons

Procedure

1. Introduce the Big Book *The Big Rig*. Read the title to the children.
2. Remind the children they have been learning about the *-ig* word family. Elicit words from the *-ig* word family before you begin.
3. Take a picture walk through the book. Label all the pictures. Tell the children what is happening using some of the text from the book.
4. Read the book to the children, modeling 1:1, directionality, and return sweep.
5. Reread the book, inviting the children to read along with you. Do this several times. Vary the activity by echo reading or choral reading.
6. Give the children their own copy of the book. Have them read the book to themselves and then color in all the pictures. Have them read the book to a partner.
7. Listen to the children read the book independently or send the books home as a "read together," depending on the reading ability of each child.

The Big Rig

Name _____

- -

It's the day of the dig on Mr. Pig's farm.

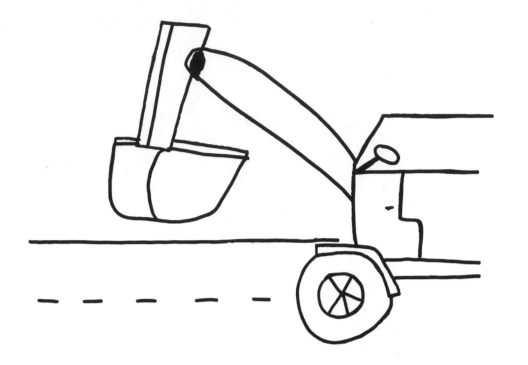

Here comes the big rig.

The big rig's ready to dig, dig, dig!

As the rig begins to dig . . .

- -

Mr. Pig wears a wig and does a jig.

"Hooray for the dig!" says the pig in the wig.

"I can roll in the mud made by the big rig."

LINE MASTER—"THE BIG RIG" BIG BOOK

LINE MASTER—"THE BIG RIG" BIG BOOK

LINE MASTER—"THE BIG RIG" BIG BOOK

LINE MASTER—"THE BIG RIG" BIG BOOK

LINE MASTER—"THE BIG RIG" BIG BOOK

Word Family

-in

Lesson 1

Objectives

- To provide exposure and an introduction to the *-in* word family
- To introduce the anchor word *pinwheel*

Materials

- Chart-sized poem "My Pinwheel"
- Chart paper
- Water-based marker

Procedure

1. Read and discuss the book *Gilberto and the Wind* by Marie Hall Ets. Brainstorm with the children different things that move or are blown by the wind. This will activate prior knowledge and fill in gaps for children with limited experience. List all responses on a piece of chart paper or chalkboard. You can also use a graphic organizer, such as the web shown here.

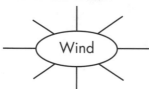

2. Tell the children you will now read a poem titled "My Pinwheel." Read "My Pinwheel" to the children. Model 1:1 by pointing to each word as you read. Invite the children to read through the poem with you the second time.

> **My Pinwheel**
>
> I hold my pinwheel into the wind.
> Around and around the colors spin.
> If there's no wind,
> how does it spin?
> **I** run like the wind and make it spin.
> My pinwheel's colors
> so bright to see—
> Watching them makes me very happy!

274

3. Vary this activity by echo reading ("My turn, your turn") and choral reading.
4. Ask the children if they can find the word *pinwheel* in the poem. Invite children to come up and circle the word *pinwheel* with a water-based marker.
5. Now do the art activity with the children, either as a small group or whole class.

Art Activity

Materials
- Line master of poem "My Pinwheel"
- Line master of pinwheel
- 12" × 18" yellow construction paper
- Stapler
- Crayons

Preparation
Reproduce the poem "My Pinwheel" and staple it to the right side of the yellow construction paper.

Procedure
1. Children color in the pinwheel.
2. Staple the pinwheel onto the yellow paper.
3. Send the poem and art activity home. This gives family members an opportunity to read the poem with the child.

Conclusion of Lesson

Bring children back to the large "My Pinwheel" poem. Reread the poem together as a class.

My Pinwheel

I hold my pinwheel into the wind.
Around and around the colors spin.
If there's no wind,
how does it spin?
I run like the wind and make it spin.
My pinwheel's colors
so bright to see—
Watching them makes me very happy!

My Pinwheel

I hold my pinwheel into the wind.
Around and around the colors spin.
If there's no wind,
how does it spin?
I run like the wind and make it spin.
My pinwheel's colors
so bright to see—
Watching them makes me very happy!

LINE MASTER—PINWHEEL

Lesson 2

Objectives

- Child will recognize -*in* words visually and auditorily.
- Child will read words that belong in the -*in* word family.

Materials

- Large copy of poem "My Robot"
- Teacher-made model of the -*in* blending strip
- Water-based marker

Procedure

1. Show children the poem "My Robot."

> **My Robot**
>
> I found some tin in a bin
> and made a robot with shiny skin.
> I press his button to begin.
> I watch him move around and spin.
> We play together every day,
> the best of friends in every way!
> We don't play to lose or win.
> Just having fun makes us grin!

2. Tell the children they are going to hear a poem about a child who made a robot out of tin.
3. Ask children what they notice about the poem.
4. Read the poem to the children.
5. Read the poem again. This time emphasize the rhyming words.
6. Remind the children that words that sound alike at the end are called rhyming words.
7. Read the poem again and have the children listen for the words that rhyme. Have the children give you a "thumbs up" (or some other "secret signal") when they hear a rhyming word.
8. Circle with the water-based marker each rhyming word as it is read.
9. Read all the circled words aloud.
10. Write the circled rhyming words from the poem in a column on a separate piece of chart paper.

11. Ask the children what they notice that is the same about the words. Anything different?

12. Show the children that the only difference in each *-in* word is the beginning sound. The middle and ending sounds are the same.

13. Ask the children for other words in the *-in* word family.

14. Show the children the *-in* blending strip and safety pin. Say "in" out loud. Tell the children you will now show them words that belong to the *-in* word family.

15. Move the blending strip to create all the *-in* word-family words. Say the words as you create them. Have the children repeat them after you. Repeat this activity several times.

16. Explain to the children they will make their own *-in* blending strip.

-in Blending Strip Activity

Materials

- Line master of safety pin
- Blending strip with letters: *b, f, p, t, w, ch, sp, gr* (You may edit the letters on the strip.)
- Blank writing paper
- Line master of *-in* word family flashcards
- Crayons
- Scissors

Procedure

1. Give children the line master of the safety pin, scissors, and crayons.

2. Children color in the safety pin.

3. Children cut out the safety pin.

4. Cut two 1-inch vertical slits to the left of the chunk printed on the blending strip. Be sure to leave a 1-inch space between the slits.

5. Slide the strip through the slits.

6. Children read all the *-in* words to you by sliding the strip through the safety pin.

7. Vary the activity by having children read to a partner, you, or any other adult.

8. Children then write all the words on the writing paper provided.

9. Send the blending strip and flashcards home to reinforce the *-in* word family.

Challenge Activity

Children will turn the writing paper over and use each of the -in words in a sentence. They can also make up a silly poem of their own using some or all of the -in words.

Reinforcement Activity

1. For a small group mini-lesson, put the magnetic letters **p i n** on an overhead projector (or on the floor facing the children if you do not have an overhead).

2. Tell children they know the word *pin*.

3. Run your finger under the word *pin* and say *p-i-n*, stretching out the word as you say it. Again, slide your finger under the word *pin* and stretch it out. Have children say it with you this time.

4. Remove the "p" from the word and tell children this chunk of the word is *in*.

5. Put a "t" in front of the -in on the overhead. Again, slide your finger under the word, stretching out *t-i-n* as you say it. Repeat this procedure with the letters *b, f, w, ch, sp,* and *gr*. Have the children practice making -in family words individually or with a partner using the magnetic letters as you demonstrated on the overhead projector.

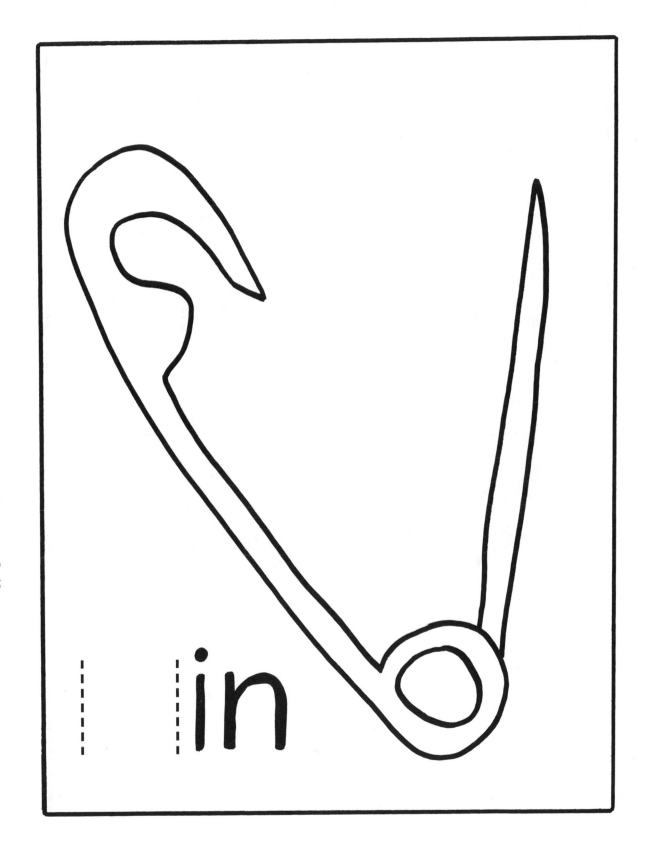

in

LINE MASTER—SAFETY PIN BLENDING STRIP

bin	fin
pin	tin
win	chin
grin	spin

Lesson 3

Objective
- Child will read *-in* words in the context of a story.

Materials
- Big Book *My Robot*
- Little Book *My Robot*
- Crayons

Procedure
1. Introduce the Big Book *My Robot.* Read the title to the children.
2. Remind the children they have been learning about the *-in* word family. Elicit words from the *-in* word family before you begin.
3. Take a picture walk through the book. Label all the pictures. Tell the children what is happening using some of the text from the book.
4. Read the book to the children, modeling 1:1, directionality, and return sweep.
5. Reread the book, inviting the children to read along with you. Do this several times. Vary the activity by echo reading or choral reading.
6. Give the children their own copy of the book. Have them read the book to themselves and then color in all the pictures. Have them read the book to a partner.
7. Listen to the children read the book independently or send the books home as a "read together," depending on the reading ability of each child.

My Robot

Name _____

- -

I found some tin in a bin . . .

and made a robot with shiny skin.

- -

I press his button to begin.

I watch him move around and spin.

Sunday Monday Tuesday
Wednesday Thursday
Friday Saturday

We play together every day,

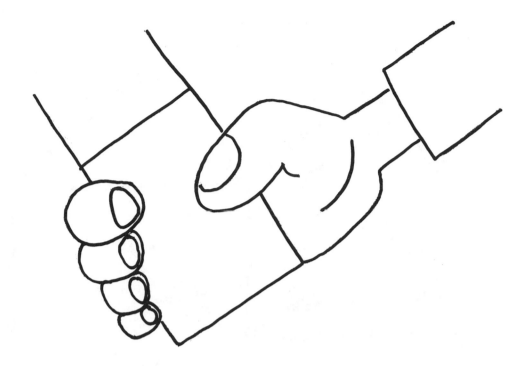

the best of friends in every way!

We don't play to lose or win.
Just having fun makes us grin!

Put your tin in this bin.

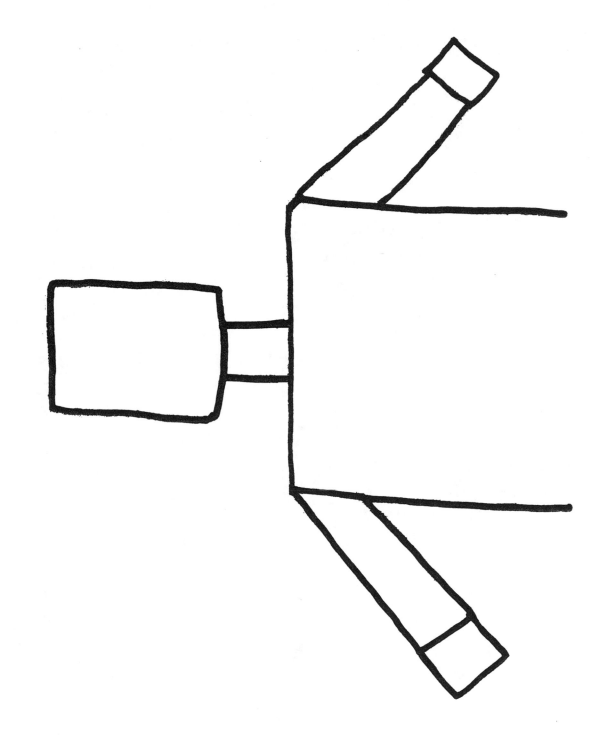

LINE MASTER—"MY ROBOT" BIG BOOK

LINE MASTER—"MY ROBOT" BIG BOOK

LINE MASTER—"MY ROBOT" BIG BOOK

Sunday Monday Tuesday
Wednesday Thursday
Friday Saturday

LINE MASTER—"MY ROBOT" BIG BOOK

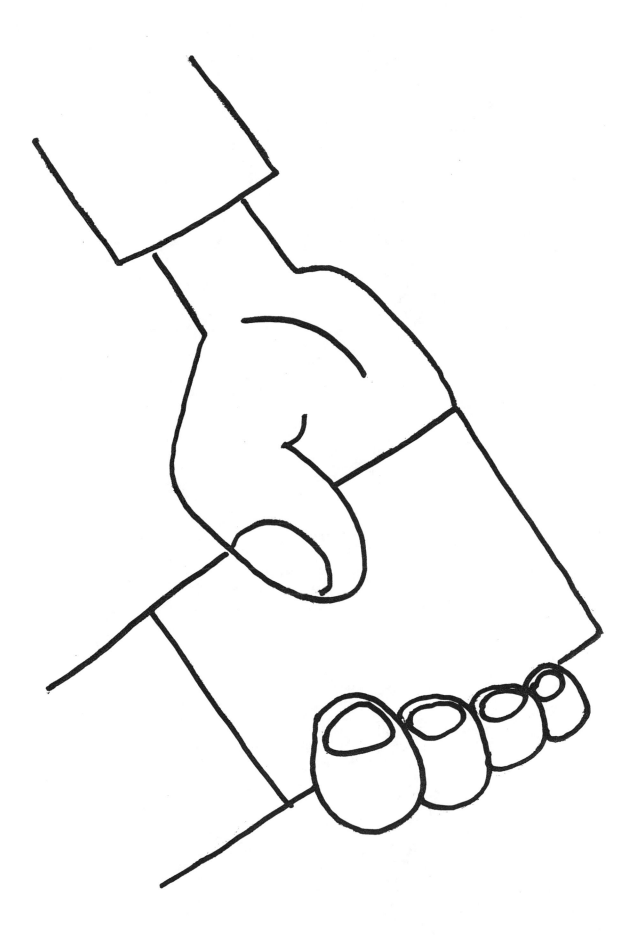

LINE MASTER—"MY ROBOT" BIG BOOK

LINE MASTER—"MY ROBOT" BIG BOOK

Word Family

•-ine

Lesson 1

Objectives

- To provide exposure and an introduction to the -ine word family
- To introduce the anchor word *shine*

Materials

- Chart-sized poem "Sparkle and Shine"
- Chart paper
- Water-based marker

Procedure

1. Read *Andrew's Loose Tooth* by Robert Munsch.
2. Discuss with children ways they can take care of their teeth.
3. Tell the children you will now read a poem titled "Sparkle and Shine." Read "Sparkle and Shine" to the children. Model 1:1 by pointing to each word as you read. Invite the children to read through the poem with you the second time.

> **Sparkle and Shine**
>
> I have a great smile . . .
> and it's all mine.
> I take care of my teeth.
> I brush them 'til they shine.
> I eat healthy foods and drink milk when I dine.
> That's why my smile does sparkle and shine.

4. Vary this activity by echo reading ("My turn, your turn") and choral reading.
5. Ask the children if they can find the word *shine* in the poem. Invite children to come up and circle the word *shine* with a water-based marker.
6. Now do the art activity with the children, either as a small group or whole class.

Art Activity

Materials

- Red water-based markers
- Line master of poem "Sparkle and Shine"
- Line master of mouth
- 12" × 18" black construction paper
- Stapler

Preparation

Reproduce the poem "Sparkle and Shine" and staple it to the right side of the black construction paper.

Procedure

1. Children color in the lips.
2. Children cut out the mouth.
3. Staple the mouth onto the black paper.
4. Send the poem and art activity home. This gives family members an opportunity to read the poem with the child.

Conclusion of Lesson

Bring children back to the large "Sparkle and Shine" poem. Reread the poem together as a class.

Sparkle and Shine

I have a great smile . . .
and it's all mine.
I take care of my teeth.
I brush them 'til they shine.
I eat healthy foods and drink milk
when I dine.
That's why my smile does sparkle
and shine.

Sparkle and Shine

I have a great smile . . .
and it's all mine.
I take care of my teeth.
I brush them 'til they shine.
I eat healthy foods and drink milk
when I dine.
That's why my smile does sparkle
and shine.

LINE MASTER—MOUTH

Lesson 2

Objectives

- Child will recognize *-ine* words visually and auditorily.
- Child will read words that belong in the *-ine* word family.

Materials

- Large copy of poem "A Mighty Fine Swine"
- Teacher-made model of the *-ine* blending strip
- Water-based marker

Procedure

1. Show children the poem "A Mighty Fine Swine."

A Mighty Fine Swine

People say I'm a dirty swine.
That doesn't bother me.
I don't whine.
I clean myself up and I'm mighty fine.
I wash and I scrub
until I shine,
from the top of my head
to my pink piggy spine.
I shine, shine, shine . . .
until I dine.
I guess I am
a dirty swine!

---

2. Tell the children they are going to hear a poem about a silly swine. Make sure the children know that a swine is another name for a pig.
3. Read the poem to the children.
4. Ask children what they notice about the poem.
5. Read the poem again. This time emphasize the rhyming words.
6. Remind the children that words that sound alike at the end are called rhyming words.
7. Read the poem again and have the children listen for the words that rhyme. Have the children give you a "thumbs up" (or some other "secret signal") when they hear a rhyming word.
8. Circle with the water-based marker each rhyming word as it is read.

9. Read all the circled words aloud.

10. Write the circled rhyming words from the poem in a column on a separate piece of chart paper.

11. Ask the children what they notice that is the same about the words. Anything different?

12. Show the children that the only difference in each -*ine* word is the beginning sound. The middle and ending sounds are the same.

13. Ask the children for other words in the -*ine* word family.

14. Show the children the -*ine* blending strip and pine. Say "ine" out loud. Tell the children you will now show them words that belong to the -*ine* word family.

15. Move the blending strip to create all the -*ine* word-family words. Say the words as you create them. Have the children repeat them after you. Repeat this activity several times.

16. Explain to the children they will make their own -*ine* blending strip.

-ine Blending Strip Activity

Materials

- Line master of pine
- Blending strip with letters: *f, m, n, d, p, v, sp, sw, sh, wh* (You may edit the letters on the strip.)
- Blank writing paper
- Line master of -*ine* word family flashcards
- Crayons
- Scissors

Procedure

1. Give children the line master of the pine, scissors, and crayons.
2. Children color in the pine.
3. Children cut out the pine.
4. Cut two 1-inch vertical slits to the left of the chunk printed on the blending strip. Be sure to leave a 1-inch space between the slits.
5. Slide the strip through the slits.
6. Children read all the -*ine* words to you by sliding the strip through the pine.
7. Vary the activity by having children read to a partner, you, or any other adult.
8. Children then write all the words on the writing paper provided.

9. Send the blending strip and flashcards home to reinforce the *-ine* word family.

Challenge Activity

Children will turn the writing paper over and use each of the *-ine* words in a sentence. They can also make up a silly poem of their own using some or all of the *-ine* words.

Reinforcement Activity

1. For a small group mini-lesson, put the magnetic letters **p i n e** on an overhead projector (or on the floor facing the children if you do not have an overhead).

2. Tell children they know the word *pine*.

3. Run your finger under the word *pine* and say *p-i-n-e*, stretching out the word as you say it. Again, slide your finger under the word *pine* and stretch it out. Have children say it with you this time.

4. Remove the "p" from the word and tell children this chunk of the word is *ine*.

5. Put an "m" in front of the *-ine* on the overhead. Again, slide your finger under the word, stretching out *m-i-n-e* as you say it. Repeat this procedure with the letters *f, n, d, v, sp, sw, wh,* and *sh*. Have the children practice making *-ine* family words individually or with a partner using the magnetic letters as you demonstrated on the overhead projector.

LINE MASTER—PINE BLENDING STRIP

fine	mine
nine	dine
pine	vine
shine	spine

Lesson 3

Objective

- Child will read *-ine* words in the context of a story.

Materials

- Big Book *A Mighty Fine Swine*
- Little Book *A Mighty Fine Swine*
- Crayons

Procedure

1. Introduce the Big Book *A Mighty Fine Swine*. Read the title to the children.

2. Remind the children they have been learning about the *-ine* word family. Elicit words from the *-ine* word family before you begin.

3. Take a picture walk through the book. Label all the pictures. Tell the children what is happening using some of the text from the book.

4. Read the book to the children, modeling 1:1, directionality, and return sweep.

5. Reread the book, inviting the children to read along with you. Do this several times. Vary the activity by echo reading or choral reading.

6. Give the children their own copy of the book. Have them read the book to themselves and then color in all the pictures. Have them read the book to a partner.

7. Listen to the children read the book independently or send the books home as a "read together," depending on the reading ability of each child.

A Mighty Fine Swine

Name _____

- -

What a dirty swine!

People say I'm a dirty swine.

That doesn't bother me. I don't whine.

I clean myself up and I'm mighty fine.

I wash and I scrub until I shine,
from the top of my head to my pink piggy spine.

I shine, shine, shine . . .

until I dine.

I guess I am a dirty swine!

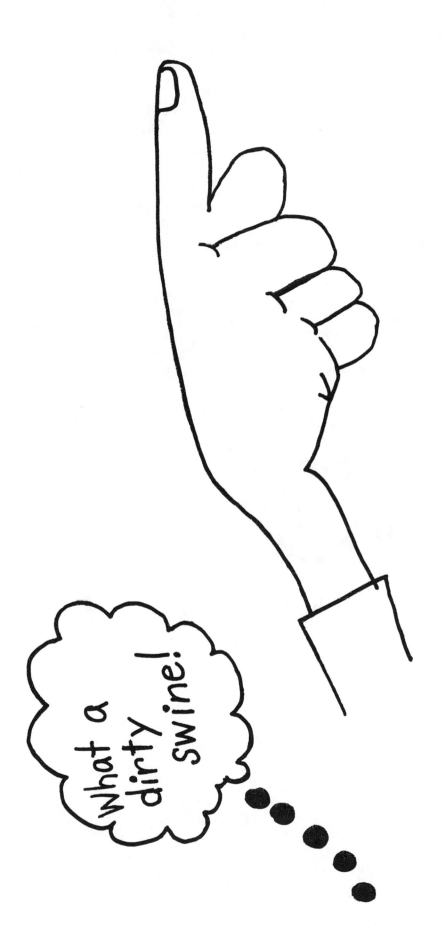

LINE MASTER—"A MIGHTY FINE SWINE" BIG BOOK

LINE MASTER—"A MIGHTY FINE SWINE" BIG BOOK

LINE MASTER—"A MIGHTY FINE SWINE" BIG BOOK

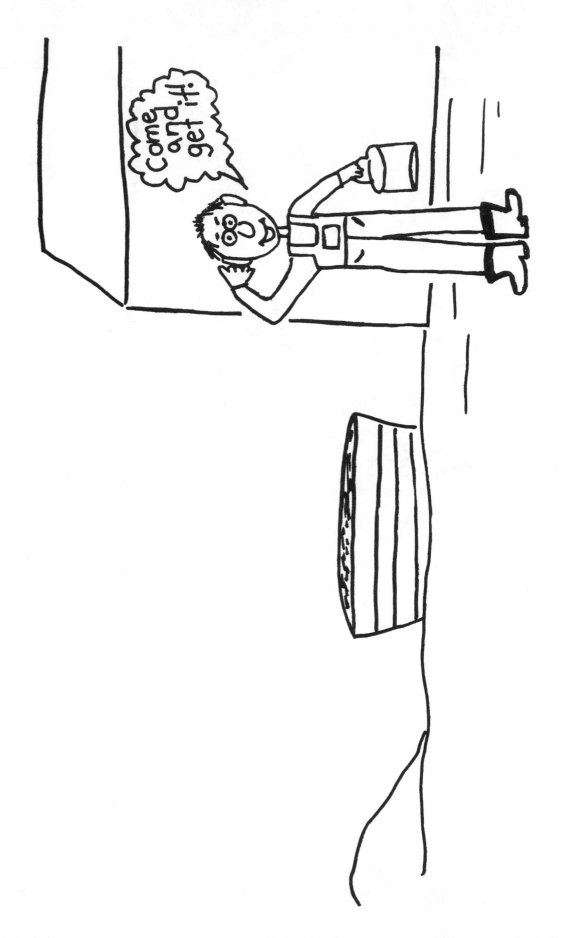

LINE MASTER—"A MIGHTY FINE SWINE" BIG BOOK

LINE MASTER—"A MIGHTY FINE SWINE" BIG BOOK

Word Family -ip

Lesson 1

Objectives

- To provide exposure and an introduction to the -*ip* word family
- To introduce the anchor word *sip*

Materials

- Chart-sized poem "The Crazy Straw"
- Chart paper
- Water-based marker

Procedure

1. Read *Chicken Soup With Rice* by Maurice Sendak. Reread the January poem. Ask children what else they can sip and how they can sip (for example, off of a spoon or through a straw).

2. Tell the children you will now read a poem titled "The Crazy Straw" to them. Model 1:1 by pointing to each word as you read. Invite the children to read through the poem with you the second time.

> **The Crazy Straw**
>
> A crazy straw is really neat
> when your drink is really sweet.
> Sip it once, sip it twice,
> a crazy straw is really nice.
> Sip it three times, sip it four.
> Sip until you have no more.

3. Vary this activity by echo reading ("My turn, your turn") and choral reading. The children will also enjoy acting out the poem using pretend mirrors.

4. Ask the children if they can find the word *sip* in the poem. Invite children to come up and circle the word *sip* with a water-based marker.

5. Now do the art activity with the children, either as a small group or whole class.

Art Activity

Materials

- Markers
- Linc master of poem "The Crazy Straw"
- Line master of crazy straw
- 12" × 18" purple construction paper
- Stapler
- Pencils

Preparation

Reproduce the poem "The Crazy Straw" and staple it to the right side of the purple construction paper.

Procedure

1. Children complete the sentence: I like to sip _____ through my crazy straw.
2. Children color in the crazy straw and drink.
3. Staple the crazy straw onto the purple paper.
4. Send the poem and art activity home. This gives family members an opportunity to read the poem with the child.

Conclusion of Lesson

Bring children back to the large "The Crazy Straw" poem. Reread the poem together as a class.

The Crazy Straw

A crazy straw is really neat
when your drink is really sweet.
Sip it once, sip it twice,
a crazy straw is really nice.
Sip it three times, sip it four.
Sip until you have no more.

The Crazy Straw

A crazy straw is really neat
when your drink is really sweet.
Sip it once, sip it twice,
a crazy straw is really nice.
Sip it three times, sip it four.
Sip until you have no more.

I like to sip _____

through my crazy straw!

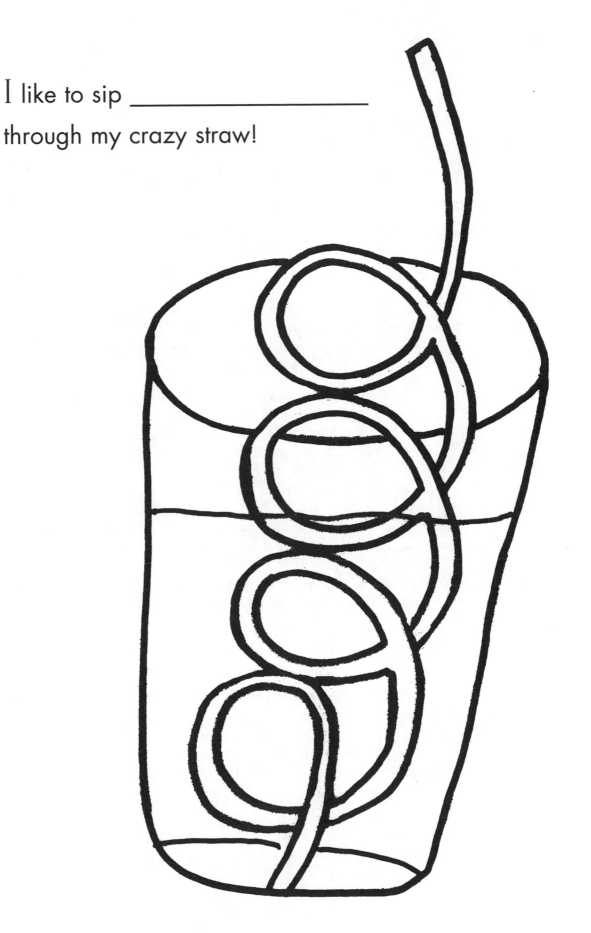

LINE MASTER—CRAZY STRAW

Lesson 2

Objectives

- Child will recognize -*ip* words visually and auditorily.
- Child will read words that belong in the -*ip* word family.

Materials

- Large copy of poem "Eddie the Elephant"
- Teacher-made model of the -*ip* blending strip
- Water-based marker

Procedure

1. Show children the poem "Eddie the Elephant."

> **Eddie the Elephant**
>
> Eddie the elephant dreamed of a trip
> on a great big tall sailing ship.
> The wind began to whip the ship.
> The waves made the ship tip and dip.
> "OH, NO! I need to get a grip!
> I hope this ship doesn't flip!"
> Eddie woke up and licked his lip.
> "Phew! That was **some** trip on the sailing ship!"

2. Tell the children they are going to hear a poem about an elephant named Eddie who took a trip on a ship.
3. Read the poem to the children.
4. Ask children what they notice about the poem.
5. Read the poem again. This time emphasize the rhyming words.
6. Remind the children that words that sound alike at the end are called rhyming words.
7. Read the poem again and have the children listen for the words that rhyme. Have the children give you a "thumbs up" (or some other "secret signal") when they hear a rhyming word.
8. Circle with the water-based marker each rhyming word as it is read.
9. Read all the circled words aloud.
10. Write the circled rhyming words from the poem in a column on a separate piece of chart paper.

11. Ask the children what they notice that is the same about the words. Anything different?

12. Show the children that the only difference in each -*ip* word is the beginning sound. The middle and ending sounds are the same.

13. Ask the children for other words in the -*ip* word family.

14. Show the children the -*ip* blending strip and ship. Say "ip" out loud. Tell the children you will now show them words that belong to the -*ip* word family.

15. Move the blending strip to create all the -*ip* word-family words. Say the words as you create them. Have the children repeat them after you. Repeat this activity several times.

16. Explain to the children they will make their own -*ip* blending strip.

-ip Blending Strip Activity

Materials

- Line master of ship
- Blending strip with letters: *d, h, l, n, p, r, s, t, z, sh* (You may edit the letters on the strip.)
- Blank writing paper
- Line master of -*ip* word family flashcards
- Crayons
- Scissors

Procedure

1. Give children the line master of the ship, scissors, and crayons.

2. Children color in the ship.

3. Children cut out the ship.

4. Cut two 1-inch vertical slits to the left of the chunk printed on the blending strip. Be sure to leave a 1-inch space between the slits.

5. Slide the strip through the slits.

6. Children read all the -*ip* words to you by sliding the strip through the ship.

7. Vary the activity by having children read to a partner, you, or any other adult.

8. Children then write all the words on the writing paper provided.

9. Send the blending strip and flashcards home to reinforce the -*ip* word family.

Challenge Activity

Children will turn the writing paper over and use each of the *-ip* words in a sentence. They can also make up a silly poem of their own using some or all of the *-ip* words.

Reinforcement Activity

1. For a small group mini-lesson, put the magnetic letters **l i p** on an overhead projector (or on the floor facing the children if you do not have an overhead).

2. Tell children they know the word *lip*.

3. Run your finger under the word *lip* and say *l-i-p*, stretching out the word as you say it. Again, slide your finger under the word *lip* and stretch it out. Have children say it with you this time.

4. Remove the "l" from the word and tell children this chunk of the word is *ip*.

5. Put an "r" in front of the *-ip* on the overhead. Again, slide your finger under the word, stretching out *r-i-p* as you say it. Repeat this procedure with the letters *d, h, n, p, s, t, z, sh*. Have the children practice making *-ip* family words individually or with a partner using the magnetic letters as you demonstrated on the overhead projector.

ip

LINE MASTER—SHIP BLENDING STRIP

dip	hip
lip	rip
sip	tip
slip	ship

Lesson 3

Objective

- Child will read -*ip* words in the context of a story.

Materials

- Big Book *Eddie the Elephant*
- Little Book *Eddie the Elephant*
- Crayons

Procedure

1. Introduce the Big Book *Eddie the Elephant*. Read the title to the children.

2. Remind the children they have been learning about the -*ip* word family. Elicit words from the -*ip* word family before you begin.

3. Take a picture walk through the book. Label all the pictures. Tell the children what is happening using some of the text from the book.

4. Read the book to the children, modeling 1:1, directionality, and return sweep.

5. Reread the book, inviting the children to read along with you. Do this several times. Vary the activity by echo reading or choral reading.

6. Give the children their own copy of the book. Have them read the book to themselves and then color in all the pictures. Have them read the book to a partner.

7. Listen to the children read the book independently or send the books home as a "read together," depending on the reading ability of each child.

Eddie the Elephant

Name _____

- -

Eddie the elephant dreamed of a trip
on a great big tall sailing ship.

The wind began to whip the ship.

The waves made the ship tip and dip.

"OH, NO! I need to get a grip!"

- -

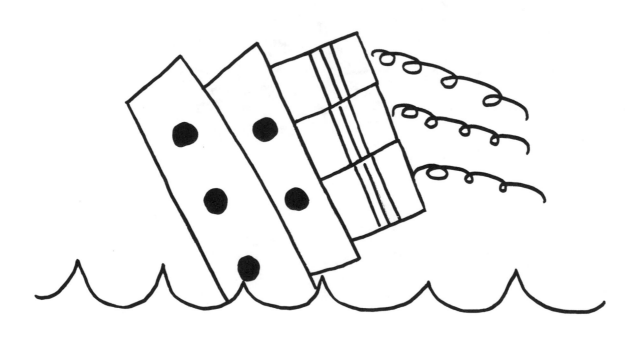

"I hope this ship doesn't flip!"

Eddie woke up and licked his lip.

- -

"Phew! That was **some** trip on a sailing ship!"

LINE MASTER—"EDDIE THE ELEPHANT" LITTLE BOOK

LINE MASTER—"EDDIE THE ELEPHANT" BIG BOOK

LINE MASTER—"EDDIE THE ELEPHANT" BIG BOOK

LINE MASTER—"EDDIE THE ELEPHANT" BIG BOOK

LINE MASTER—"EDDIE THE ELEPHANT" BIG BOOK

LINE MASTER—"EDDIE THE ELEPHANT" BIG BOOK

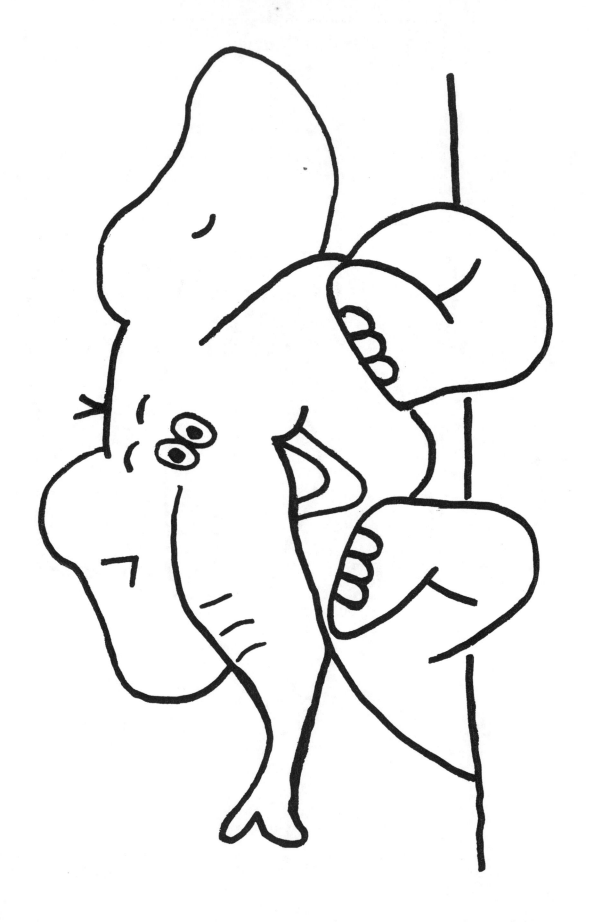

LINE MASTER—"EDDIE THE ELEPHANT" BIG BOOK

-it

Lesson 1

Objectives

- To provide exposure and an introduction to the *-it* word family
- To introduce the anchor word *fit*

Materials

- Chart-sized poem "Does It Fit?"
- Chart paper
- Water-based marker

Procedure

1. Read and discuss the book *Froggy Gets Dressed* by Jonathan London. Review with the children the many different kinds of clothing Froggy puts on. Ask the children if they have ever gone to put on a piece of clothing only to find out it did not fit anymore. Ask children to share their experiences regarding that topic.

2. Tell the children you will now read a poem titled "Does It Fit?" Read "Does It Fit?" to the children. Model 1:1 by pointing to each word as you read. Invite the children to read through the poem with you the second time.

Does It Fit?

Are my arms too long?
Or did they grow?
My shirt doesn't fit.
OH, NO!
Are my legs too long?
Or did they grow?
My pants don't fit.
OH, NO!
"Mom," I call, "come look and see!
None of my clothes fit me!"

---

3. Vary this activity by echo reading ("My turn, your turn") and choral reading. The children will also enjoy acting out the poem using pretend mirrors.

4. Ask the children if they can find the word *fit* in the poem. Invite children to come up and circle the word *fit* with a water-based marker.

5. Now do the art activity with the children, either as a small group or whole class.

Art Activity

Materials
- Line master of poem "Does It Fit?"
- Line master of child
- 12" × 18" red construction paper
- Stapler
- Crayons

Preparation
Reproduce the poem "Does It Fit?" and staple it to the right side of the red construction paper.

Procedure
1. Children color in the child.
2. Staple the child onto the red paper.
3. Send the poem and art activity home. This gives family members an opportunity to read the poem with the child.

Conclusion of Lesson

Bring children back to the large "Does It Fit?" poem. Reread the poem together as a class.

Does It Fit?

Are my arms too long?
Or did they grow?
My shirt doesn't fit.
OH, NO!
Are my legs too long?
Or did they grow?
My pants don't fit.
OH, NO!
"Mom," I call, "come look and see!
None of my clothes fit me!"

Does It Fit?

Are my arms too long?
Or did they grow?
My shirt doesn't fit.
OH, NO!
Are my legs too long?
Or did they grow?
My pants don't fit.
OH, NO!
"Mom," I call, "come look and see!
None of my clothes fit me!"

Copyright © 2003 by Roberta Seckler Brown and Susan Carey

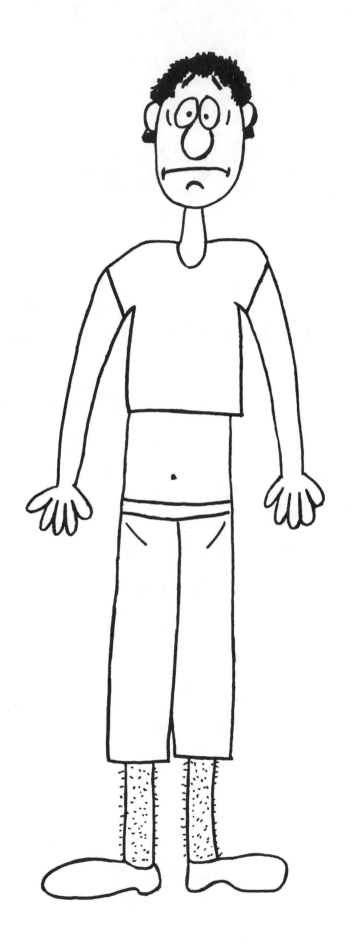

LINE MASTER—CHILD

Lesson 2

Objectives

- Child will recognize -*it* words visually and auditorily.
- Child will read words that belong in the -*it* word family.

Materials

- Large copy of poem "How to Make a Banana Split"
- Teacher-made model of the -*it* blending strip
- Water-based marker

Procedure

1. Show children the poem "How to Make a Banana Split."

> **How to Make a Banana Split**
>
> Choose a banana for your split,
> not too big or it won't fit.
> Peel it carefully,
> then make a slit.
> Keep on going,
> it's no time to quit.
> You've got to finish your banana split.
> Now add the ice cream, and whipped cream, too!
> Add a cherry on top.
> You're still not through!
> Add syrup and nuts.
> Now you're done!
> Sit down and eat it!
> Banana splits are fun!

2. Tell the children they are going to hear a poem about how to make a banana split.
3. Ask children what they notice about the poem.
4. Read the poem to the children.
5. Read the poem again. This time emphasize the rhyming words.
6. Remind the children that words that sound alike at the end are called rhyming words.
7. Read the poem again and have the children listen for the words that rhyme. Have the children give you a "thumbs up" (or some other "secret signal") when they hear a rhyming word.

8. Circle with the water-based marker each rhyming word as it is read.

9. Read all the circled words aloud.

10. Write the circled rhyming words from the poem in a column on a separate piece of chart paper.

11. Ask the children what they notice that is the same about the words. Anything different?

12. Show the children that the only difference in each -it word is the beginning sound. The middle and ending sounds are the same.

13. Ask the children for other words in the -it word family.

14. Show the children the -it blending strip and banana split. Say "it" out loud. Tell the children you will now show them words that belong to the -it word family.

15. Move the blending strip to create all the -it word-family words. Say the words as you create them. Have the children repeat them after you. Repeat this activity several times.

16. Explain to the children they will make their own -it blending strip.

-it Blending Strip Activity

Materials

- Line master of banana split
- Blending strip with letters: *b, f, h, k, l, p, s, w, sl* (You may edit the letters on the strip.)
- Blank writing paper
- Line master of -it word family flashcards
- Crayons
- Scissors

Procedure

1. Give children the line master of the banana split, scissors, and crayons.

2. Children color in the banana split.

3. Children cut out the banana split.

4. Cut two 1-inch vertical slits to the left of the chunk printed on the blending strip. Be sure to leave a 1-inch space between the slits.

5. Slide the strip through the slits.

6. Children read all the -it words to you by sliding the strip through the banana split.

7. Vary the activity by having children read to a partner, you, or any other adult.

8. Children then write all the words on the writing paper provided.

9. Send the blending strip and flashcards home to reinforce the *-it* word family.

Challenge Activity

Children will turn the writing paper over and use each of the *-it* words in a sentence. They can also make up a silly poem of their own using some or all of the *-it* words.

Reinforcement Activity

1. For a small group mini-lesson, put the magnetic letters **f i t** on an overhead projector (or on the floor facing the children if you do not have an overhead).

2. Tell children they know the word *fit.*

3. Run your finger under the word *fit* and say *f-i-t,* stretching out the word as you say it. Again, slide your finger under the word *fit* and stretch it out. Have children say it with you this time.

4. Remove the "f" from the word and tell children this chunk of the word is *it.*

5. Put an "s" in front of the *-it* on the overhead. Again, slide your finger under the word, stretching out *s-i-t* as you say it. Repeat this procedure with the letters *b, h, l, p, w, k, sl.* Have the children practice making *-it* family words individually or with a partner using the magnetic letters as you demonstrated on the overhead projector.

LINE MASTER—BANANA SPLIT BLENDING STRIP

bit	fit
hit	kit
lit	pit
sit	slit

Lesson 3

Objective

- Child will read -*it* words in the context of a story.

Materials

- Big Book *How to Make a Banana Split*
- Little Book *How to Make a Banana Split*
- Crayons

Procedure

1. Introduce the Big Book *How to Make a Banana Split*. Read the title to the children.

2. Remind the children they have been learning about the -*it* word family. Elicit words from the -*it* word family before you begin.

3. Take a picture walk through the book. Label all the pictures. Tell the children what is happening using some of the text from the book.

4. Read the book to the children, modeling 1:1, directionality, and return sweep.

5. Reread the book, inviting the children to read along with you. Do this several times. Vary the activity by echo reading or choral reading.

6. Give the children their own copy of the book. Have them read the book to themselves and then color in all the pictures. Have them read the book to a partner.

7. Listen to the children read the book independently or send the books home as a "read together," depending on the reading ability of each child.

How to Make a Banana Split

Name _____

- -

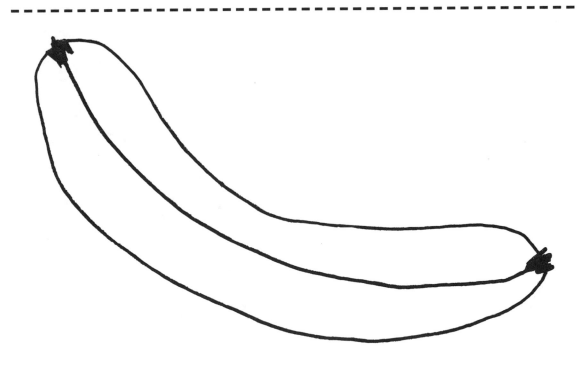

Choose a banana for your split,
not too big or it won't fit.

Peel it carefully, then make a slit.
Keep on going, it's no time to quit.

- -

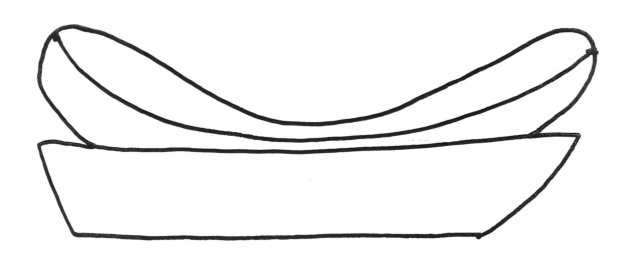

You've got to finish your banana split.

Now add ice cream, and whipped cream, too!

- -

Add a cherry on top. You're still not through!

LINE MASTER—"HOW TO MAKE A BANANA SPLIT" LITTLE BOOK

Add syrup and nuts. Now you're done!

Sit down and eat it! Banana splits are fun!

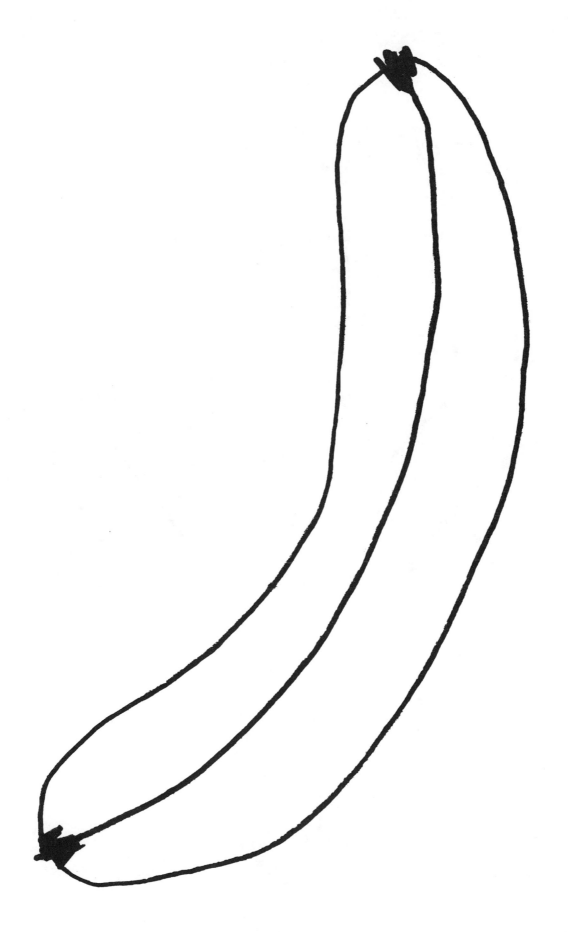

LINE MASTER—"HOW TO MAKE A BANANA SPLIT" BIG BOOK

LINE MASTER—"HOW TO MAKE A BANANA SPLIT" BIG BOOK

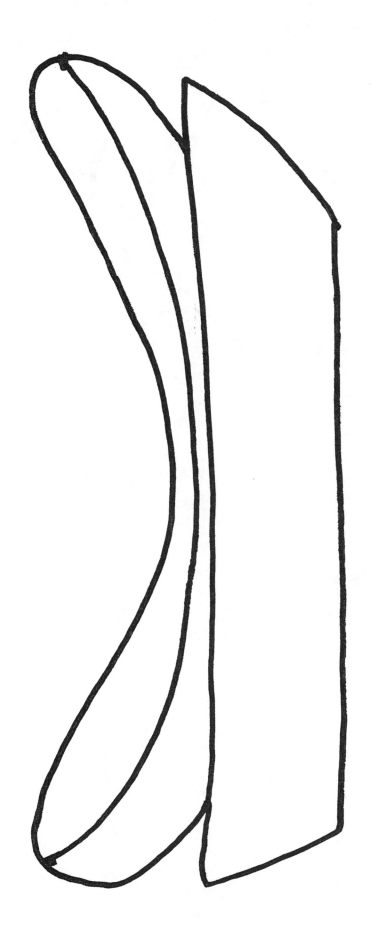

LINE MASTER—"HOW TO MAKE A BANANA SPLIT" BIG BOOK

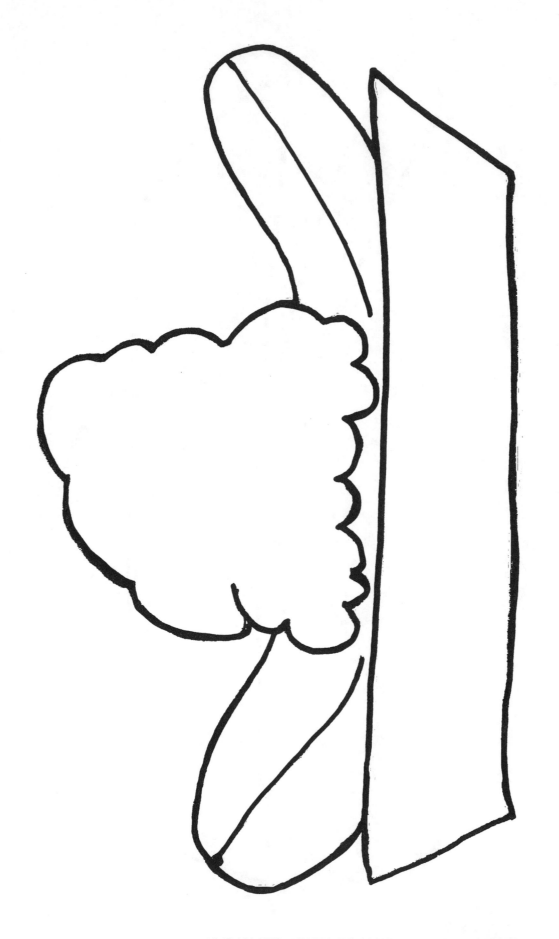

LINE MASTER—"HOW TO MAKE A BANANA SPLIT" BIG BOOK

LINE MASTER—"HOW TO MAKE A BANANA SPLIT" BIG BOOK

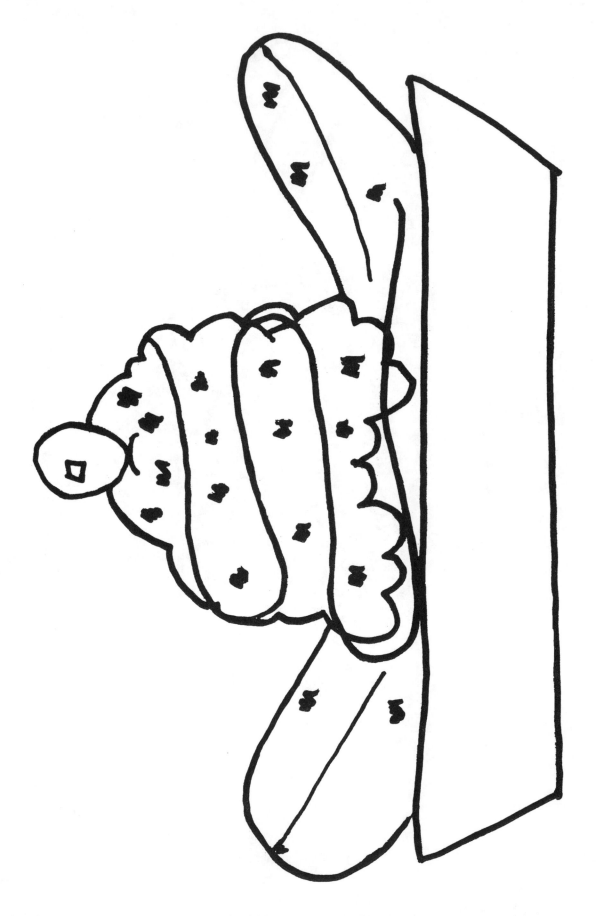

LINE MASTER—"HOW TO MAKE A BANANA SPLIT" BIG BOOK

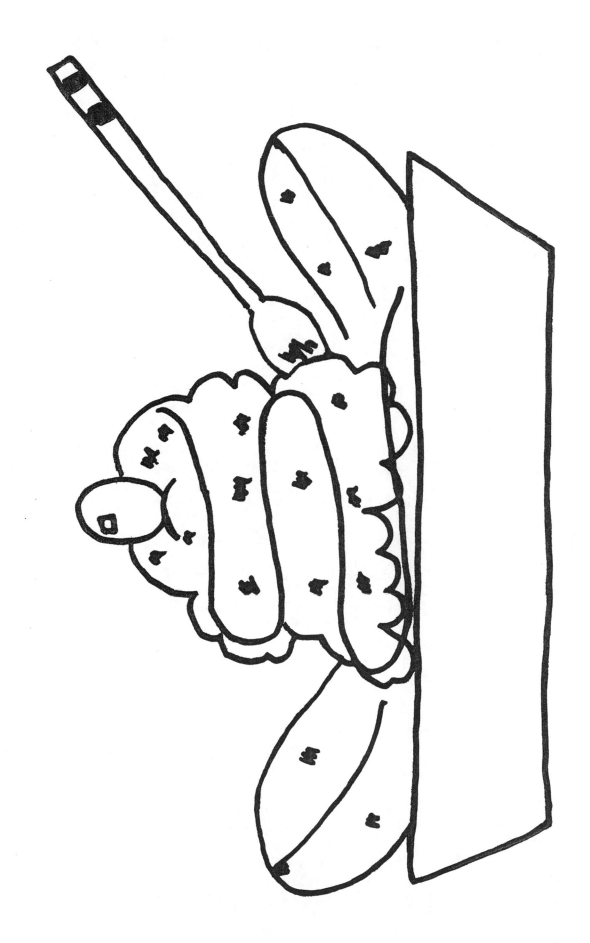

LINE MASTER—"HOW TO MAKE A BANANA SPLIT" BIG BOOK

Word Family

-og

Lesson 1

Objectives

- To provide exposure and an introduction to the -og word family
- To introduce the anchor word *hog*

Materials

- Chart-sized poem "Book Hog"
- Chart paper
- Water-based marker

Procedure

1. Brainstorm with children all the different types of books there are. This will activate prior knowledge and fill in gaps for children. List all responses on a piece of chart paper or chalkboard. You can also use a graphic organizer, such as the web shown here.

2. Tell the children you will now read a poem titled "Book Hog." Read "Book Hog" to the children. Model 1:1 by pointing to each word as you read. Invite the children to read through the poem with you the second time.

Book Hog

I'm a book hog—
books are my thing.
I can't get enough—
I read everything!
I read to learn
and just for fun.
I read everything
under the sun!
I'm a book hog. How about you?
Read lots of books . . .
You can be one, too!

3. Vary this activity by echo reading ("My turn, your turn") and choral reading.

4. Ask the children if they can find the word *hog* in the poem. Invite children to come up and circle the word *hog* with a water-based marker.

5. Now do the art activity with the children, either as a small group or whole class.

Art Activity

Materials

- Scissors
- Crayons
- Line master of poem "Book Hog"
- Line master of book
- 12" × 18" blue construction paper
- Stapler
- Pencils

Preparation

Reproduce the poem "Book Hog" and staple it to the right side of the blue construction paper.

Procedure

1. Children complete the sentence: My favorite book is _____.
2. Children color the book.
3. Children cut out the book.
4. Staple the book onto the blue paper.
5. Send the poem and art activity home. This gives family members an opportunity to read the poem with the child.

Conclusion of Lesson

Bring children back to the large "Book Hog" poem. Reread the poem together as a class.

Book Hog

I'm a book hog—
books are my thing.
I can't get enough—
I read everything!
I read to learn
and just for fun.
I read everything
under the sun!
I'm a book hog. How about you?
Read lots of books . . .
You can be one, too!

- -

Book Hog

I'm a book hog—
books are my thing.
I can't get enough—
I read everything!
I read to learn
and just for fun.
I read everything
under the sun!
I'm a book hog. How about you?
Read lots of books . . .
You can be one, too!

My favorite book is . . .

Lesson 2

Objectives

- Child will recognize -*og* words visually and auditorily.
- Child will read words that belong in the -*og* word family.

Materials

- Large copy of poem "Little Frog"
- Teacher-made model of the -*og* blending strip
- Water-based marker

Procedure

1. Show children the poem "Little Frog."

Little Frog

Once there was a little frog
who would always jog down by the bog.
He liked to rest on the bumpy log.
How he loved to sit on his log in the bog.
One day when he went out to jog,
he found there was a lot of fog.
"I can't jog in all this fog!
I'll just sit and rest on the bumpy log."

---

2. Tell the children they are going to hear a poem about a little frog.
3. Read the poem to the children.
4. Ask children what they notice about the poem.
5. Read the poem again. This time emphasize the rhyming words.
6. Remind the children that words that sound alike at the end are called rhyming words.
7. Read the poem again and have the children listen for the words that rhyme. Have the children give you a "thumbs up" (or some other "secret signal") when they hear a rhyming word.
8. Circle with the water-based marker each rhyming word as it is read.
9. Read all the circled words aloud.
10. Write the circled rhyming words from the poem in a column on a separate piece of chart paper.
11. Ask the children what they notice that is the same about the words. Anything different?

12. Show the children that the only difference in each *-og* word is the beginning sound. The middle and ending sounds are the same.
13. Ask the children for other words in the *-og* word family.
14. Show the children the *-og* blending strip and log. Say "og" out loud. Tell the children you will now show them words that belong to the *-og* word family.
15. Move the blending strip to create all the *-og* word-family words. Say the words as you create them. Have the children repeat them after you. Repeat this activity several times.
16. Explain to the children they will make their own *-og* blending strip.

-og Blending Strip Activity

Materials
- Line master of log
- Blending strip with letters: *b, d, f, h, l, j, fr, sm* (You may edit the letters on the strip.)
- Blank writing paper
- Line master of *-og* word family flashcards
- Crayons
- Scissors

Procedure
1. Give children the line master of the log, scissors, and crayons.
2. Children color in the log.
3. Children cut out the log.
4. Cut two 1-inch vertical slits to the left of the chunk printed on the blending strip. Be sure to leave a 1-inch space between the slits.
5. Slide the strip through the slits.
6. Children read all the *-og* words to you by sliding the strip through the log.
7. Vary the activity by having children read to a partner, you, or any other adult.
8. Children then write all the words on the writing paper provided.
9. Send the blending strip and flashcards home to reinforce the *-og* word family.

Challenge Activity
Children will turn the writing paper over and use each of the *-og* words in a sentence. They can also make up a silly poem of their own using some or all of the *-og* words.

Reinforcement Activity

1. For a small group mini-lesson, put the magnetic letters **l o g** on an overhead projector (or on the floor facing the children if you do not have an overhead).

2. Tell children they know the word *log*.

3. Run your finger under the word *log* and say *l-o-g*, stretching out the word as you say it. Again, slide your finger under the word *log* and stretch it out. Have children say it with you this time.

4. Remove the "l" from the word and tell children this chunk of the word is *og*.

5. Put a "j" in front of the *-og* on the overhead. Again, slide your finger under the word, stretching out *j-o-g* as you say it. Repeat this procedure with the letters *b, d, f, h, fr, sm.* Have the children practice making *-og* family words individually or with a partner using the magnetic letters as you demonstrated on the overhead projector.

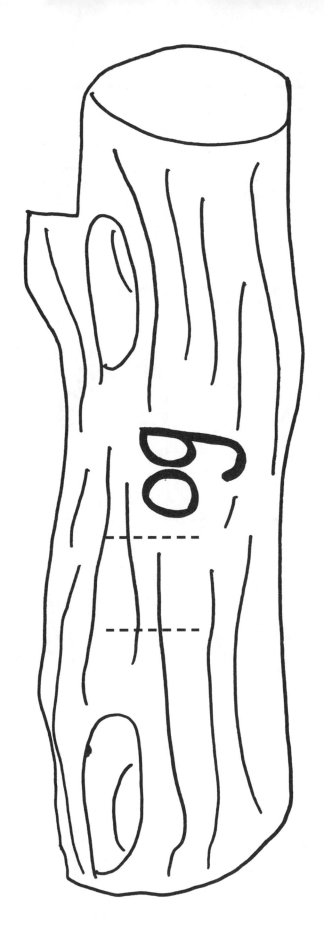

LINE MASTER—LOG BLENDING STRIP

bog	dog
fog	hog
log	jog
frog	smog

LINE MASTER—OG WORD FAMILY FLASHCARDS

Lesson 3

Objective

- Child will read -og words in the context of a story.

Materials

- Big Book *Little Frog*
- Little Book *Little Frog*
- Crayons

Procedure

1. Introduce the Big Book *Little Frog*. Read the title to the children.
2. Remind the children they have been learning about the -og word family. Elicit words from the -og word family before you begin.
3. Take a picture walk through the book. Label all the pictures. Tell the children what is happening using some of the text from the book.
4. Read the book to the children, modeling 1:1, directionality, and return sweep.
5. Reread the book, inviting the children to read along with you. Do this several times. Vary the activity by echo reading or choral reading.
6. Give the children their own copy of the book. Have them read the book to themselves and then color in all the pictures. Have them read the book to a partner.
7. Listen to the children read the book independently or send the books home as a "read together," depending on the reading ability of each child.

Little Frog

Name _____

- -

Once there was a little frog
who would always jog down by the bog.

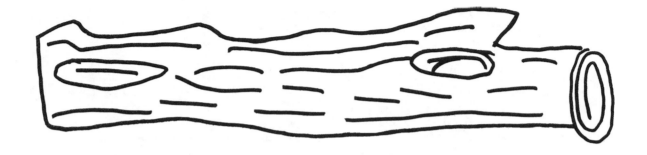

He liked to rest on the bumpy log.

- -

How he loved to sit on his log in the bog.

LINE MASTER—"LITTLE FROG" LITTLE BOOK

One day when he went out to jog,

he found there was a lot of fog.

"I can't jog in all this fog!"

"I'll just sit and rest on the bumpy log."

LINE MASTER—"LITTLE FROG" BIG BOOK

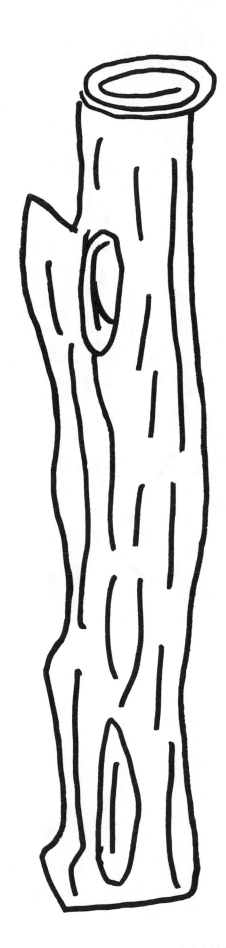

LINE MASTER—"LITTLE FROG" BIG BOOK

LINE MASTER—"LITTLE FROG" BIG BOOK

LINE MASTER—"LITTLE FROG" BIG BOOK

LINE MASTER—"LITTLE FROG" BIG BOOK

LINE MASTER—"LITTLE FROG" BIG BOOK

LINE MASTER—"LITTLE FROG" BIG BOOK

Word Family

-ook

Lesson 1

Objectives

- To provide exposure and an introduction to the -*ook* word family
- To introduce the anchor word *look*

Materials

- Chart-sized poem "Look!"
- Chart paper
- Water-based marker

Procedure

1. Brainstorm with children all the things you can see or look at. This will activate prior knowledge and fill in gaps for children. List all responses on a piece of chart paper or chalkboard. You can also use a graphic organizer, such as the web shown here.

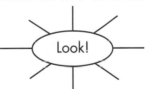

2. Tell the children you will now read a poem titled "Look!" Read "Look!" to the children. Model 1:1 by pointing to each word as you read. Invite the children to read through the poem with you the second time.

> **Look!**
>
> I look at a book.
> I look at a tree.
> I look at a flower.
> I look at a bee.
> But . . . I look in a mirror,
> and what do I see?
> I see a face,
> a face that is me!

3. Vary this activity by echo reading ("My turn, your turn") and choral reading. The children will also enjoy acting out the poem using pretend mirrors.

4. Ask the children if they can find the word *look* in the poem. Invite children to come up and circle the word *look* with a water-based marker.

5. Now do the art activity with the children, either as a small group or whole class.

Art Activity

Materials
- Scissors
- Crayons
- Line master of poem "Look!"
- Line master of mirror
- 6" × 9" blue construction paper
- 8-inch circle of metallic silver shiny paper
- Stapler
- Glue

Preparation
Reproduce the poem "Look!" and staple it to the right side of the blue construction paper.

Procedure
1. Children color the handle of the mirror first.
2. Children cut out the outline of the handle and the mirror.
3. Glue the shiny silver circle onto the mirror.
4. Staple the mirror onto the blue paper.
5. Let dry.
6. Send the poem and art activity home. This gives family members an opportunity to read the poem with the child.

Conclusion of Lesson

Bring children back to the large "Look!" poem. Reread the poem together as a class.

Look!

I look at a book.
I look at a tree.
I look at a flower.
I look at a bee.
But . . . I look in a mirror,
and what do I see?
I see a face,
a face that is me!

Look!

I look at a book.
I look at a tree.
I look at a flower.
I look at a bee.
But . . . I look in a mirror,
and what do I see?
I see a face,
a face that is me!

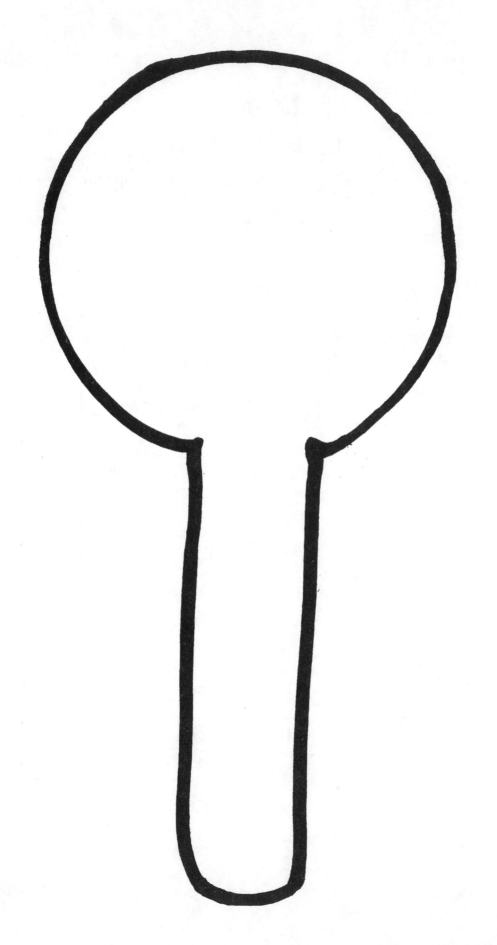

LINE MASTER—MIRROR

Lesson 2

Objectives

- Child will recognize -ook words visually and auditorily.
- Child will read words that belong in the -ook word family.

Materials

- Large copy of poem "A Silly Cook"
- Teacher-made model of the -ook blending strip
- Water-based marker

Procedure

1. Show children the poem "A Silly Cook."

> **A Silly Cook**
>
> A silly cook took a look
> at a "how-to-do-it" helpful book.
> "Ahh ha!" said the silly cook.
> "This book can teach me how to cook
> some chewy, gooey, yummy gook!"
> He took his pot and . . .
> shook! shook! shook!
> "Oh, no!" shouted the silly cook.
> "It's on my hat—this nasty gook!"
> And that's what happened
> when he took
> a book to teach him
> how to cook!

2. Tell the children they are going to hear a poem about a silly cook.
3. Read the poem to the children.
4. Ask children what they notice about the poem.
5. Read the poem again. This time emphasize the rhyming words.
6. Remind the children that words that sound alike at the end are called rhyming words.
7. Read the poem again and have the children listen for the words that rhyme. Have the children give you a "thumbs up" (or some other "secret signal") when they hear a rhyming word.
8. Circle with the water-based marker each rhyming word as it is read.

9. Read all the circled words aloud.

10. Write the circled rhyming words from the poem in a column on a separate piece of chart paper.

11. Ask the children what they notice that is the same about the words. Anything different?

12. Show the children that the only difference in each -ook word is the beginning sound. The middle and ending sounds are the same.

13. Ask the children for other words in the -ook word family.

14. Show the children the -ook blending strip and book. Say "ook" out loud. Tell the children you will now show them words that belong to the -ook word family.

15. Move the blending strip to create all the -ook word-family words. Say the words as you create them. Have the children repeat them after you. Repeat this activity several times.

16. Explain to the children they will make their own -ook blending strip.

-ook Blending Strip Activity

Materials

- Line master of book
- Blending strip with letters: *b, h, c, t, l, n, r, g, sh* (You may edit the letters on the strip.)
- Blank writing paper
- Line master of -ook word family flashcards
- Crayons
- Scissors

Procedure

1. Give children the line master of the book, scissors, and crayons.

2. Children color in the book.

3. Children cut out the book.

4. Cut two 1-inch vertical slits to the left of the chunk printed on the blending strip. Be sure to leave a 1-inch space between the slits.

5. Slide the strip through the slits.

6. Children read all the -ook words to you by sliding the strip through the book.

7. Vary the activity by having children read to a partner, you, or any other adult.

8. Children then write all the words on the writing paper provided.

9. Send the blending strip and flashcards home to reinforce the -*ook* word family.

Challenge Activity

Children will turn the writing paper over and use each of the -*ook* words in a sentence. They can also make up a silly poem of their own using some or all of the -*ook* words.

Reinforcement Activity

1. For a small group mini-lesson, put the magnetic letters **l o o k** on an overhead projector (or on the floor facing the children if you do not have an overhead).

2. Tell children they know the word *look.*

3. Run your finger under the word *look* and say *l-o-o-k*, stretching out the word as you say it. Again, slide your finger under the word *look* and stretch it out. Have children say it with you this time.

4. Remove the "l" from the word and tell children this chunk of the word is *ook.*

5. Put a "t" in front of the -*ook* on the overhead. Again, slide your finger under the word, stretching out *t-o-o-k* as you say it. Repeat this procedure with the letters *b, h, c, n, r, g, sh.*

6. Have the children practice making -*ook* family words individually or with a partner using the magnetic letters as you demonstrated on the overhead projector.

ook

LINE MASTER—BOOK BLENDING STRIP

book	hook
cook	took
look	nook
rook	shook

Lesson 3

Objective

- Child will read -*ook* words in the context of a story.

Materials

- Big Book *A Silly Cook*
- Little Book *A Silly Cook*
- Crayons

Procedure

1. Introduce the Big Book *A Silly Cook*. Read the title to the children.

2. Remind the children they have been learning about the -*ook* word family. Elicit words from the -*ook* word family before you begin.

3. Take a picture walk through the book. Label all the pictures. Tell the children what is happening using some of the text from the book.

4. Read the book to the children, modeling 1:1, directionality, and return sweep.

5. Reread the book, inviting the children to read along with you. Do this several times. Vary the activity by echo reading or choral reading.

6. Give the children their own copy of the book. Have them read the book to themselves and then color in all the pictures. Have them read the book to a partner.

7. Listen to the children read the book independently or send the books home as a "read together," depending on the reading ability of each child.

A Silly Cook

Name _____

A silly cook took a look at
a "how-to-do-it" helpful book.

"Ahh ha!" said the silly cook.

- -

"This book can teach me how to cook
some chewy, gooey, yummy gook!"

He took his pot and . . . shook! shook! shook!

"Oh, no!" shouted the silly cook.

"It's on my hat—this nasty gook!"

And that's what happened when he took a book
to teach him how to cook!

LINE MASTER—"A SILLY COOK" BIG BOOK

LINE MASTER—"A SILLY COOK" BIG BOOK

LINE MASTER—"A SILLY COOK" BIG BOOK

LINE MASTER—"A SILLY COOK" BIG BOOK

LINE MASTER—"A SILLY COOK" BIG BOOK

LINE MASTER—"A SILLY COOK" BIG BOOK

Word Family

-op

Lesson 1

Objectives

- To provide exposure and an introduction to the *-op* word family
- To introduce the anchor word *stop*

Materials

- Chart-sized poem "Stop!"
- Chart paper
- Water-based marker

Procedure

1. Read and discuss the book *Go, Dog, Go!* by P. D. Eastman. Reread pages 40–45 to the children. Draw a traffic light on chart paper or the chalkboard. Ask children to tell you what the colors red, yellow, and green mean. Ask children why we need traffic lights. You want the children to understand that if there were no traffic lights, driving and crossing the street would not be safe.

2. Tell the children you will now read a poem titled "Stop!" Read "Stop!" to the children. Model 1:1 by pointing to each word as you read. Invite the children to read through the poem with you the second time.

> **Stop!**
>
> Red light, Stop!
> Green light, Go!
> Yellow light tells me to Go Slow.
> I have to stop.
> But—
> I want to go.
> I'd better slow down . . . Oh, no!

3. Vary this activity by echo reading ("My turn, your turn") and choral reading.

4. Ask the children if they can find the word *stop* in the poem. Invite children to come up and circle the word *stop* with a water-based marker.

5. Now do the art activity with the children, either as a small group or whole class.

Art Activity

Materials
- Line master of poem "Stop!"
- Line master of traffic light
- 12" × 18" blue construction paper
- Stapler
- Crayons

Preparation
Reproduce the poem "Stop!" and staple it to the right side of the blue construction paper.

Procedure
1. Children color the traffic light.
2. Staple the traffic light onto the blue paper.
3. Send the poem and art activity home. This gives family members an opportunity to read the poem with the child.

Conclusion of Lesson

Bring children back to the large "Stop!" poem. Reread the poem together as a class.

Stop!

Red light, Stop!
Green light, Go!
Yellow light tells me to Go Slow.
I have to stop.
But—
I want to go.
I'd better slow down . . . Oh, no!

Stop!

Red light, Stop!
Green light, Go!
Yellow light tells me to Go Slow.
I have to stop.
But—
I want to go.
I'd better slow down . . . Oh, no!

LINE MASTER—TRAFFIC LIGHT

Lesson 2

Objectives

- Child will recognize -*op* words visually and auditorily.
- Child will read words that belong in the -*op* word family.

Materials

- Large copy of poem "The Hippity-Hop"
- Teacher-made model of the -*op* blending strip
- Water-based marker

Procedure

1. Show children the poem "The Hippity-Hop."

The Hippity-Hop

Grab your partner and spin like a top.
That's how you do the hippity-hop!
Left foot—bip!
Right foot—bop!
That's how you do the hippity-hop!
Left hand—clip!
Right hand—clop!
That's how you do the hippity-hop!
Bip! Bop! Clip! Clop!
Keep on going—don't you stop!
Bip! Bop! Clip! Clop!
That's how you do the hippity-hop!

---

2. Tell children this is a poem about a funny dance called the Hippity-Hop.
3. Ask children what they notice about the poem.
4. Read the poem to the children.
5. Read the poem again. This time emphasize the rhyming words.
6. Remind the children that words that sound alike at the end are called rhyming words.
7. Read the poem again and have the children listen for the words that rhyme. Have the children give you a "thumbs up" (or some other "secret signal") when they hear a rhyming word.
8. Circle with the water-based marker each rhyming word as it is read.

9. Read all the circled words aloud.
10. Write the circled rhyming words from the poem in a column on a separate piece of chart paper.
11. Ask the children what they notice that is the same about the words. Anything different?
12. Show the children that the only difference in each -op word is the beginning sound. The middle and ending sounds are the same.
13. Ask the children for other words in the -op word family.
14. Show the children the -op blending strip and stop sign. Say "op" out loud. Tell the children you will now show them words that belong to the -op word family.
15. Move the blending strip to create all the -op word-family words. Say the words as you create them. Have the children repeat them after you. Repeat this activity several times.
16. Explain to the children they will make their own -op blending strip.

-op Blending Strip Activity

Materials

- Line master of stop sign
- Blending strip with letters: *b, h, m, p, t, cl, ch, st* (You may edit the letters on the strip.)
- Blank writing paper
- Line master of -op word family flashcards
- Crayons
- Scissors

Procedure

1. Give children the line master of the stop sign, scissors, and crayons.
2. Children color in the stop sign.
3. Children cut out the stop sign.
4. Cut two 1-inch vertical slits to the left of the chunk printed on the blending strip. Be sure to leave a 1-inch space between the slits.
5. Slide the strip through the slits.
6. Children read all the -op words to you by sliding the strip through the stop sign.
7. Vary the activity by having children read to a partner, you, or any other adult.

8. Children then write all the words on the writing paper provided.

9. Send the blending strip and flashcards home to reinforce the -*op* word family.

Challenge Activity

Children will turn the writing paper over and use each of the -*op* words in a sentence. They can also make up a silly poem of their own using some or all of the -*op* words.

Reinforcement Activity

1. For a small group mini-lesson, put the magnetic letters **h-o-p** on an overhead projector (or on the floor facing the children if you do not have an overhead).

2. Tell children they know the word *hop.*

3. Run your finger under the word *hop* and say *h-o-p,* stretching out the word as you say it. Again, slide your finger under the word *hop* and stretch it out. Have children say it with you this time.

4. Remove the "h" from the word and tell children this chunk of the word is *op.*

5. Put a "t" in front of the -*op* on the overhead. Again, slide your finger under the word, stretching out *t-o-p* as you say it. Repeat this procedure with the letters *b, m, p, cl, ch, st.* Have the children practice making -*op* family words individually or with a partner using the magnetic letters as you demonstrated on the overhead projector.

LINE MASTER—STOP SIGN BLENDING STRIP

bop	hop
mop	pop
top	clop
chop	stop

LINE MASTER—*OP* WORD FAMILY FLASHCARDS

Lesson 3

Objective

- Child will read -*op* words in the context of a story.

Materials

- Big Book *The Hippity-Hop*
- Little Book *The Hippity-Hop*
- Crayons

Procedure

1. Introduce the Big Book *The Hippity-Hop*. Read the title to the children.
2. Remind the children they have been learning about the -*op* word family. Elicit words from the -*op* word family before you begin.
3. Take a picture walk through the book. Label all the pictures. Tell the children what is happening using some of the text from the book.
4. Read the book to the children, modeling 1:1, directionality, and return sweep.
5. Reread the book, inviting the children to read along with you. Do this several times. Vary the activity by echo reading or choral reading.
6. Give the children their own copy of the book. Have them read the book to themselves and then color in all the pictures. Have them read the book to a partner.
7. Listen to the children read the book independently or send the books home as a "read together," depending on the reading ability of each child.

The Hippity-Hop

Name _____

- -

Grab your partner and spin like a top.
That's how you do the hippity-hop!

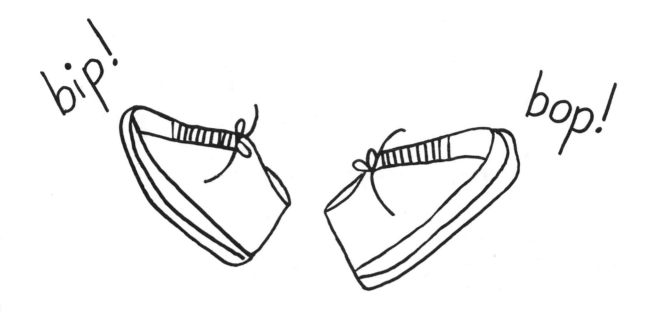

Left foot—bip! Right foot—bop!

That's how you do the hippity-hop!

LINE MASTER—"THE HIPPITY-HOP" LITTLE BOOK

Left hand—clip! Right hand—clop!

- -

That's how you do the hippity-hop!

LINE MASTER—"THE HIPPITY-HOP" LITTLE BOOK

bip! bop! clip! clop!
bip! bop! clip! clop!

Bip! Bop! Clip! Clop!
Keep on going—don't you stop!

Bip! Bop! Clip! Clop!
That's how you do the hippity-hop!

LINE MASTER—"THE HIPPITY-HOP" BIG BOOK

bop!

big!

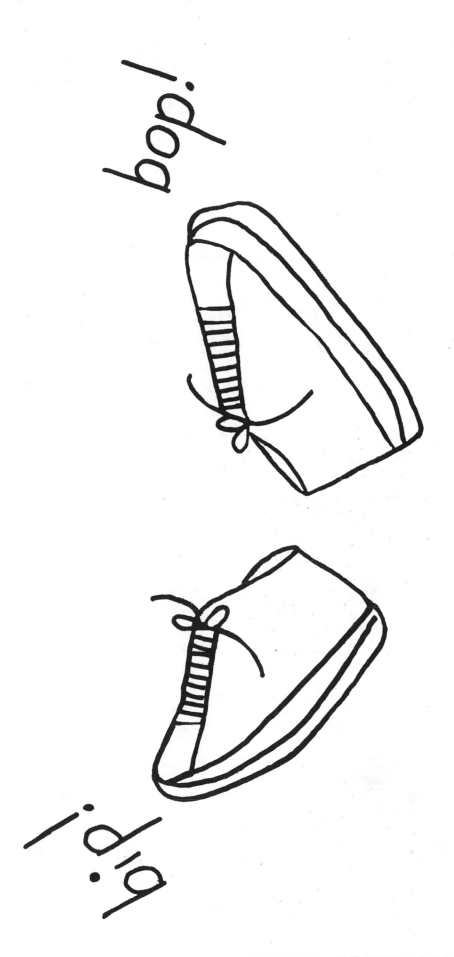

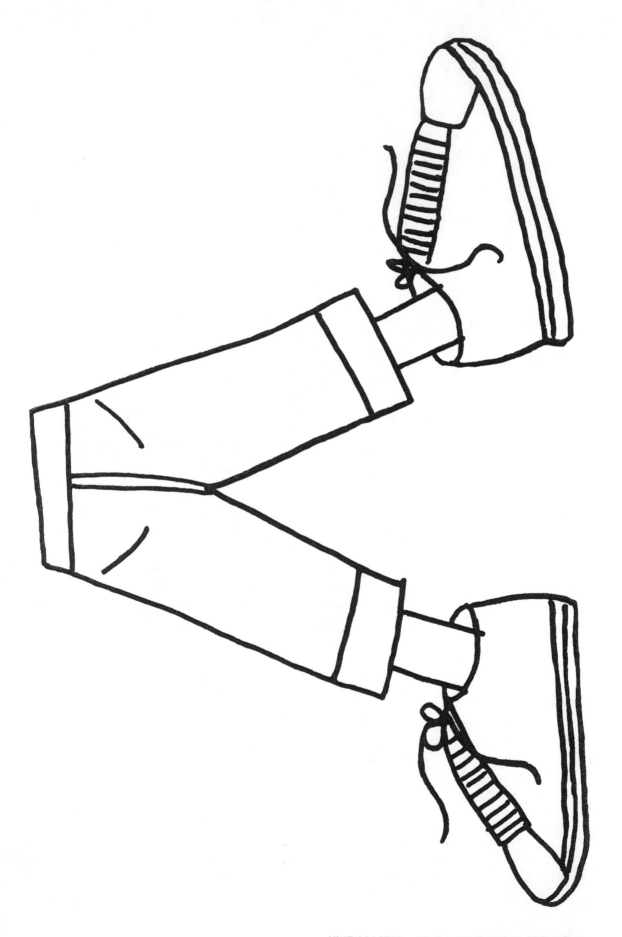

LINE MASTER—"THE HIPPITY-HOP" BIG BOOK

LINE MASTER—"THE HIPPITY-HOP" BIG BOOK

LINE MASTER—"THE HIPPITY-HOP" BIG BOOK

LINE MASTER—"THE HIPPITY-HOP" BIG BOOK

Word Family
-ot

Lesson 1

Objectives

- To provide exposure and an introduction to the *-ot* word family
- To introduce the anchor word *spot*

Materials

- Chart-sized poem "My Dog Spot"
- Chart paper
- Water-based marker

Procedure

1. Read the book *Harry the Dirty Dog* by Gene Zion.
2. Discuss the story with the children.
3. Tell the children you will now read a poem about another dog who runs away. The poem is titled "My Dog Spot." Read "My Dog Spot" to the children. Model 1:1 by pointing to each word as you read. Invite the children to read through the poem with you the second time.

> **My Dog Spot**
>
> Have you seen my dog Spot?
> He runs away quite a lot.
> He hides in places I don't see.
> I find him when he barks for me.
> We hug each other when he's found.
> My dog Spot is quite a hound!

4. Vary this activity by echo reading ("My turn, your turn") and choral reading.
5. Ask the children if they can find the word *spot* in the poem. Invite children to come up and circle the word *spot* with a water-based marker.
6. Now do the art activity with the children, either as a small group or whole class.

Art Activity

Materials

- Scissors
- Crayons
- Line master of poem "My Dog Spot"
- Line master of dog
- 12" × 18" orange construction paper
- Stapler
- Pencils

Preparation

Reproduce the poem "My Dog Spot." Hold the orange construction paper vertically and staple the poem to the top of the orange construction paper.

Procedure

1. Children color the dog.
2. Children cut out the dog.
3. Staple the dog to the left side of the poem.
4. Send the poem and art activity home. This gives family members an opportunity to read the poem with the child.

Conclusion of Lesson

Bring children back to the large "My Dog Spot" poem. Reread the poem together as a class.

My Dog Spot

Have you seen my dog Spot?
He runs away quite a lot.
He hides in places I don't see.
I find him when he barks for me.
We hug each other when he's found.
My dog Spot is quite a hound!

My Dog Spot

Have you seen my dog Spot?
He runs away quite a lot.
He hides in places I don't see.
I find him when he barks for me.
We hug each other when he's found.
My dog Spot is quite a hound!

LINE MASTER—DOG

Lesson 2

Objectives

- Child will recognize -ot words visually and auditorily.
- Child will read words that belong in the -ot word family.

Materials

- Large copy of poem "The Dot"
- Teacher-made model of the -ot blending strip
- Water-based marker

Procedure

1. Show children the poem "The Dot."

> **The Dot**
>
> You may think a dot is just a spot.
> But if you look really hard you may find it's not.
> From a simple dot you can make a lot.
> Look at the pot. Can you see the dot?
> How about the tot? Can you see the dot?
> Now it's your turn. Jot down a dot.
> Look at the dot. What have YOU got?

2. Tell the children they are going to hear a poem about what you can make with a simple dot.
3. Read the poem to the children.
4. Ask children what they notice about the poem.
5. Read the poem again. This time emphasize the rhyming words.
6. Remind the children that words that sound alike at the end are called rhyming words.
7. Read the poem again and have the children listen for the words that rhyme. Have the children give you a "thumbs up" (or some other "secret signal") when they hear a rhyming word.
8. Circle with the water-based marker each rhyming word as it is read.
9. Read all the circled words aloud.
10. Write the circled rhyming words from the poem in a column on a separate piece of chart paper.
11. Ask the children what they notice that is the same about the words. Anything different?

12. Show the children that the only difference in each -ot word is the beginning sound. The middle and ending sounds are the same.
13. Ask the children for other words in the -ot word family.
14. Show the children the -ot blending strip and pot. Say "ot" out loud. Tell the children you will now show them words that belong to the -ot word family.
15. Move the blending strip to create all the -ot word-family words. Say the words as you create them. Have the children repeat them after you. Repeat this activity several times.
16. Explain to the children they will make their own -ot blending strip.

-ot Blending Strip Activity

Materials

- Line master of pot
- Blending strip with letters: c, d, g, h, l, n, p, r, t, j, tr, sp, sh, cl, sl, pl (You may edit the letters on the strip.)
- Blank writing paper
- Line master of -ot word family flashcards
- Crayons
- Scissors

Procedure

1. Give children the line master of the pot, scissors, and crayons.
2. Children color in the pot.
3. Children cut out the pot.
4. Cut two 1-inch vertical slits to the left of the chunk printed on the blending strip. Be sure to leave a 1-inch space between the slits.
5. Slide the strip through the slits.
6. Children read all the -ot words to you by sliding the strip through the pot.
7. Vary the activity by having children read to a partner, you, or any other adult.
8. Children then write all the words on the writing paper provided.
9. Send the blending strip and flashcards home to reinforce the -ot word family.

Challenge Activity

Children will turn the writing paper over and use each of the -ot words in a sentence. They can also make up a silly poem of their own using some or all of the -ot words.

Reinforcement Activity

1. For a small group mini-lesson, put the magnetic letters **p o t** on an overhead projector (or on the floor facing the children if you do not have an overhead).

2. Tell children they know the word *pot.*

3. Run your finger under the word *pot* and say *p-o-t,* stretching out the word as you say it. Again, slide your finger under the word *pot* and stretch it out. Have children say it with you this time.

4. Remove the "p" from the word and tell children this chunk of the word is *ot.*

5. Put a "g" in front of the *-ot* on the overhead. Again, slide your finger under the word, stretching out *g-o-t* as you say it. Repeat this procedure with the letters *c, d, h, l, n, r, t, j, tr, sp, sh, sl, cl, pl.* Have the children practice making *-ot* family words individually or with a partner using the magnetic letters as you demonstrated on the overhead projector.

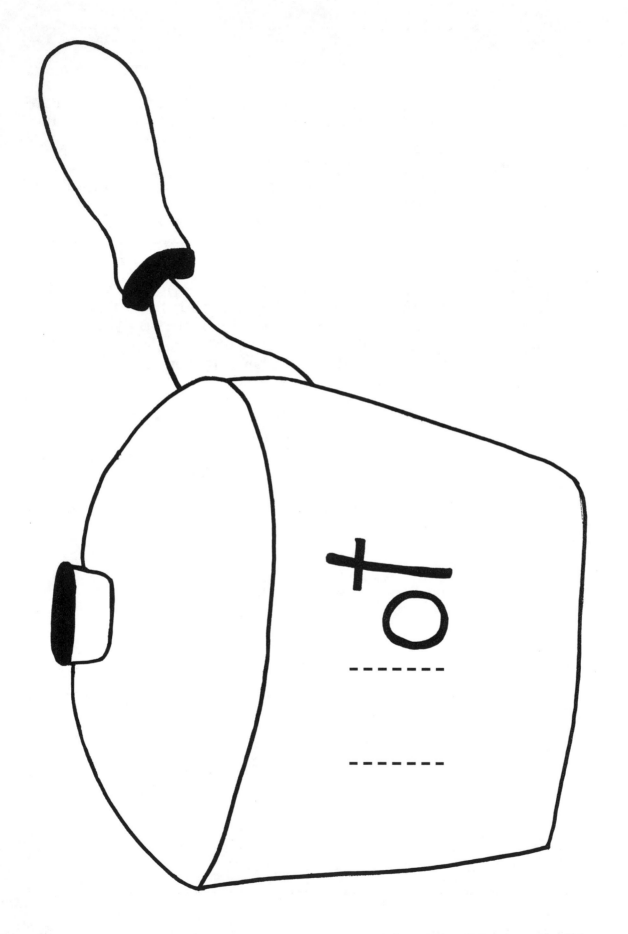

LINE MASTER—POT BLENDING STRIP

cot	dot
got	hot
lot	not
pot	slot

Lesson 3

Objective

- Child will read -*ot* words in the context of a story.

Materials

- Big Book *The Dot*
- Little Book *The Dot*
- Crayons

Procedure

1. Introduce the Big Book *The Dot*. Read the title to the children.

2. Remind the children they have been learning about the -*ot* word family. Elicit words from the -*ot* word family before you begin.

3. Take a picture walk through the book. Label all the pictures. Tell the children what is happening using some of the text from the book. On the last page of the book, elicit from the children what they could make from a dot.

4. Read the book to the children, modeling 1:1, directionality, and return sweep.

5. Reread the book, inviting the children to read along with you. Do this several times. Vary the activity by echo reading or choral reading.

6. Give the children their own copy of the book. Have them read the book to themselves and then color in all the pictures. Have them read the book to a partner.

7. Listen to the children read the book independently or send the books home as a "read together," depending on the reading ability of each child.

The Dot

Name _____

- -

You may think a dot is just a spot.

But if you look really hard you may find it's not.

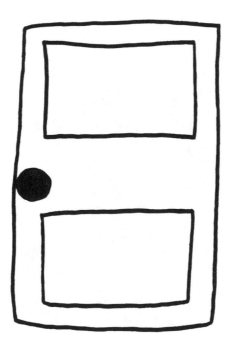

From a simple dot you can make a lot.

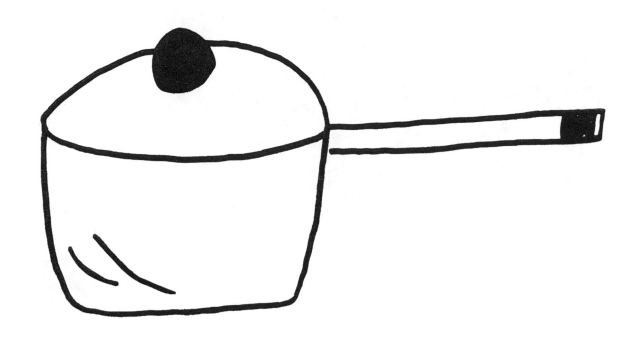

Look at the pot. Can you see the dot?

How about the tot? Can you see the dot?

Now it's your turn. Jot down a dot.

- -

Look at the dot. What have YOU got?

LINE MASTER—"THE DOT" BIG BOOK

LINE MASTER—"THE DOT" BIG BOOK

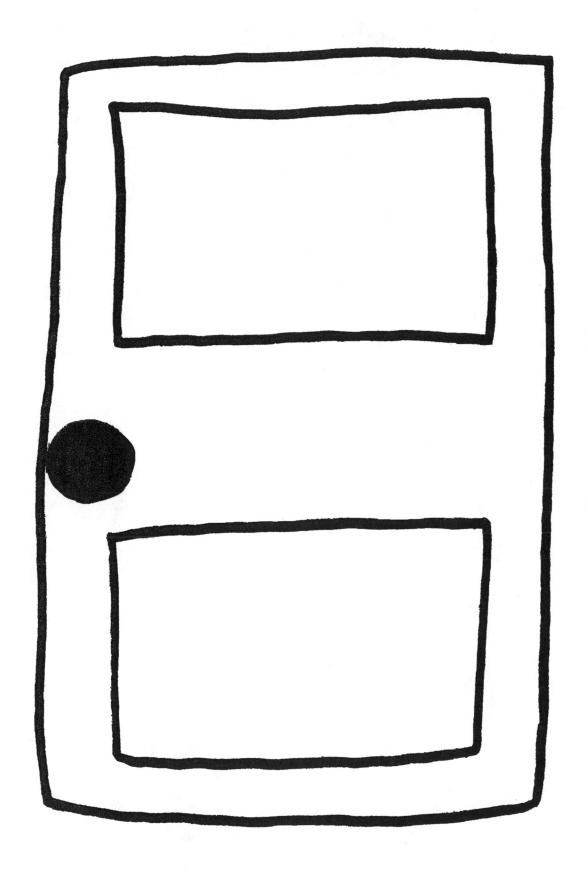

LINE MASTER—"THE DOT" BIG BOOK

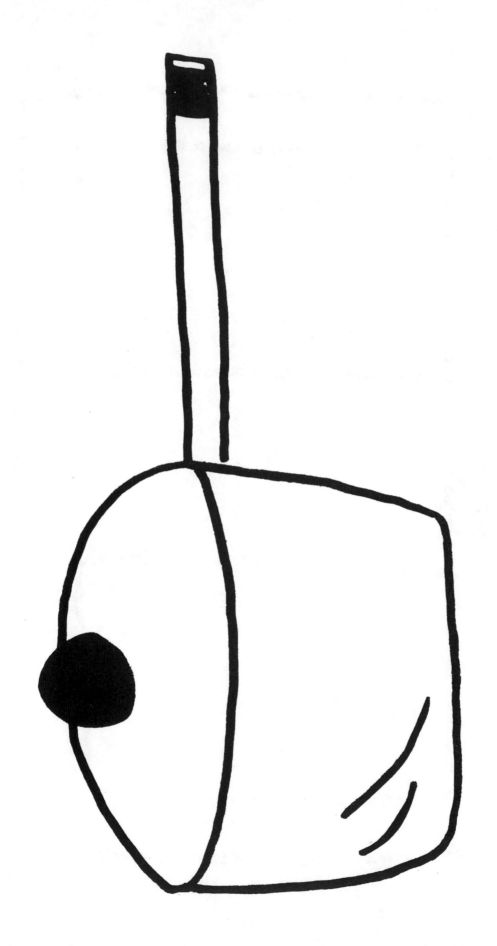

LINE MASTER—"THE DOT" BIG BOOK

LINE MASTER—"THE DOT" BIG BOOK

LINE MASTER—"THE DOT" BIG BOOK

Word Family

-ug

Lesson 1

Objectives

- To provide exposure and an introduction to the -ug word family
- To introduce the anchor word tug

Materials

- Chart-sized poem "Tug of War"
- Chart paper
- Water-based marker

Procedure

1. Ask children if they have ever played the game tug of war. Have a few children role-play the game. This will activate prior knowledge and fill in gaps for children.

2. Tell the children you will now read a poem titled "Tug of War." Read "Tug of War" to the children. Model 1:1 by pointing to each word as you read. Invite the children to read through the poem with you the second time.

> **Tug of War**
>
> It takes two teams to play the game.
> Tug of war is its name.
> Don't let go.
> Hold on tight.
> Hold that rope with all your might.
> Pull together as a team.
> It's not as easy as it may seem.
> Win or lose—did you have fun?
> Tug of war is number 1!

3. Vary this activity by echo reading ("My turn, your turn") and choral reading.

4. Ask the children if they can find the word *tug* in the poem. Invite children to come up and circle the word *tug* with a water-based marker.

5. Now do the art activity with the children, either as a small group or whole class.

Art Activity

Materials

- Markers
- Line master of poem "Tug of War"
- Line master of children
- 12" × 18" green construction paper
- Stapler
- 2-inch squares of assorted color tissue paper
- Glue

Preparation

Reproduce the poem "Tug of War." Hold the green construction paper vertically and staple the poem to the top of the green construction paper.

Procedure

1. Children color in the children.
2. Children roll the tissue squares into balls. Glue these onto the "rope line."
3. Let dry.
4. Staple the line master onto the green paper.
5. Send the poem and art activity home. This gives family members an opportunity to read the poem with the child.

Conclusion of Lesson

Bring children back to the large "Tug of War" poem. Read the poem together as a class.

Tug of War

It takes two teams to play the game.
Tug of war is its name.
Don't let go.
Hold on tight.
Hold that rope with all your might.
Pull together as a team.
It's not as easy as it may seem.
Win or lose—did you have fun?
Tug of war is number 1!

Tug of War

It takes two teams to play the game.
Tug of war is its name.
Don't let go.
Hold on tight.
Hold that rope with all your might.
Pull together as a team.
It's not as easy as it may seem.
Win or lose—did you have fun?
Tug of war is number 1!

LINE MASTER—CHILDREN

Lesson 2

Objectives

- Child will recognize *-ug* words visually and auditorily.
- Child will read words that belong in the *-ug* word family.

Materials

- Large copy of poem "The Smug Bug"
- Teacher-made model of the *-ug* blending strip
- Water-based marker

Procedure

1. Show children the poem "The Smug Bug."

The Smug Bug

Once there was a smug little bug,
who found a mug that was left on the rug.
"Hmmm," thought the smug little bug.
"I'd love to chug what's in that mug."
The smug little bug climbed into the mug,
took a sip, then swallowed,
glug, glug, glug.
"I like what I found in that mug on the rug,"
said the smug little bug.

---

2. Tell the children they are going to hear a poem about a smug little bug.
3. Read the poem to the children.
4. Ask children what they notice about the poem.
5. Read the poem again. This time emphasize the rhyming words.
6. Remind the children that words that sound alike at the end are called rhyming words.
7. Read the poem again and have the children listen for the words that rhyme. Have the children give you a "thumbs up" (or some other "secret signal") when they hear a rhyming word.
8. Circle with the water-based marker each rhyming word as it is read.
9. Read all the circled words aloud.
10. Write the circled rhyming words from the poem in a column on a separate piece of chart paper.

11. Ask the children what they notice that is the same about the words. Anything different?

12. Show the children that the only difference in each -*ug* word is the beginning sound. The middle and ending sounds are the same.

13. Ask the children for other words in the -*ug* word family.

14. Show the children the -*ug* blending strip and bug. Say "ug" out loud. Tell the children you will now show them words that belong to the -*ug* word family.

15. Move the blending strip to create all the -*ug* word-family words. Say the words as you create them. Have the children repeat them after you. Repeat this activity several times.

16. Explain to the children they will make their own -*ug* blending strip.

-ug Blending Strip Activity

Materials

* Line master of bug
* Blending strip with letters: *b, j, l, d, m, r, t, ch, gl, sl* (You may edit the letters on the strip.)
* Blank writing paper
* Line master of -*ug* word family flashcards
* Crayons
* Scissors

Procedure

1. Give children the line master of the bug, scissors, and crayons.
2. Children color in the bug.
3. Children cut out the bug.
4. Cut two 1-inch vertical slits to the left of the chunk printed on the blending strip. Be sure to leave a 1-inch space between the slits.
5. Slide the strip through the slits.
6. Children read all the -*ug* words to you by sliding the strip through the bug.
7. Vary the activity by having children read to a partner, you, or any other adult.
8. Children then write all the words on the writing paper provided.
9. Send the blending strip and flashcards home to reinforce the -*ug* word family.

Challenge Activity

Children will turn the writing paper over and use each of the *-ug* words in a sentence. They can also make up a silly poem of their own using some or all of the *-ug* words.

Reinforcement Activity

1. For a small group mini-lesson, put the magnetic letters **b u g** on an overhead projector (or on the floor facing the children if you do not have an overhead).

2. Tell children they know the word *bug.*

3. Run your finger under the word *bug* and say *b-u-g*, stretching out the word as you say it. Again, slide your finger under the word *bug* and stretch it out. Have children say it with you this time.

4. Remove the "b" from the word and tell children this chunk of the word is *ug.*

5. Put an "m" in front of the *-ug* on the overhead. Again, slide your finger under the word, stretching out *m-u-g* as you say it. Repeat this procedure with the letters *d, j, l, r, t, ch, gl, pl, sl.* Have the children practice making *-ug* family words individually or with a partner using the magnetic letters as you demonstrated on the overhead projector.

LINE MASTER—BUG BLENDING STRIP

bug	jug
hug	dug
mug	rug
tug	chug

LINE MASTER—*UG* WORD FAMILY FLASHCARDS

Lesson 3

Objective

- Child will read -ug words in the context of a story.

Materials

- Big Book *The Smug Bug*
- Little Book *The Smug Bug*
- Crayons

Procedure

1. Introduce the Big Book *The Smug Bug*. Read the title to the children.

2. Remind the children they have been learning about the -ug word family. Elicit words from the -ug word family before you begin.

3. Take a picture walk through the book. Label all the pictures. Tell the children what is happening using some of the text from the book.

4. Read the book to the children, modeling 1:1, directionality, and return sweep.

5. Reread the book, inviting the children to read along with you. Do this several times. Vary the activity by echo reading or choral reading.

6. Give the children their own copy of the book. Have them read the book to themselves and then color in all the pictures. Have them read the book to a partner.

7. Listen to the children read the book independently or send the books home as a "read together," depending on the reading ability of each child.

The Smug Bug

Name _____

- -

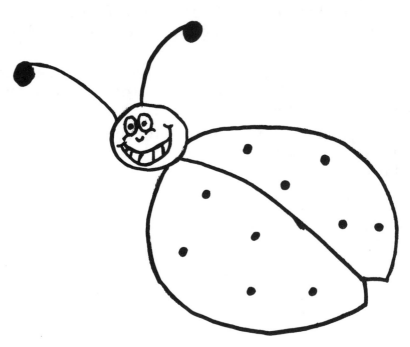

Once there was a smug little bug,

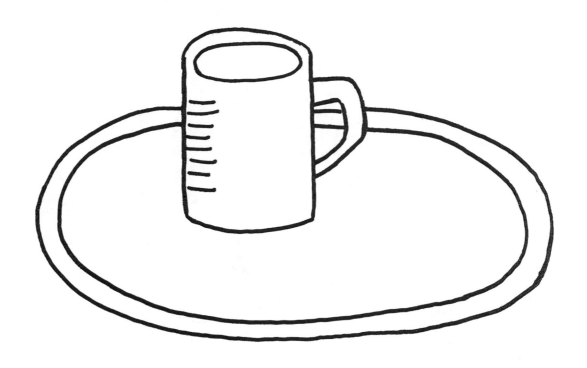

who found a mug that was left on the rug.

- -

"Hmmm," thought the smug little bug.

"I'd love to chug what's in that mug."

The smug little bug climbed into the mug,

took a sip, then swallowed, glug, glug, glug.

- -

"I like what I found in that mug on the rug,"
said the smug little bug.

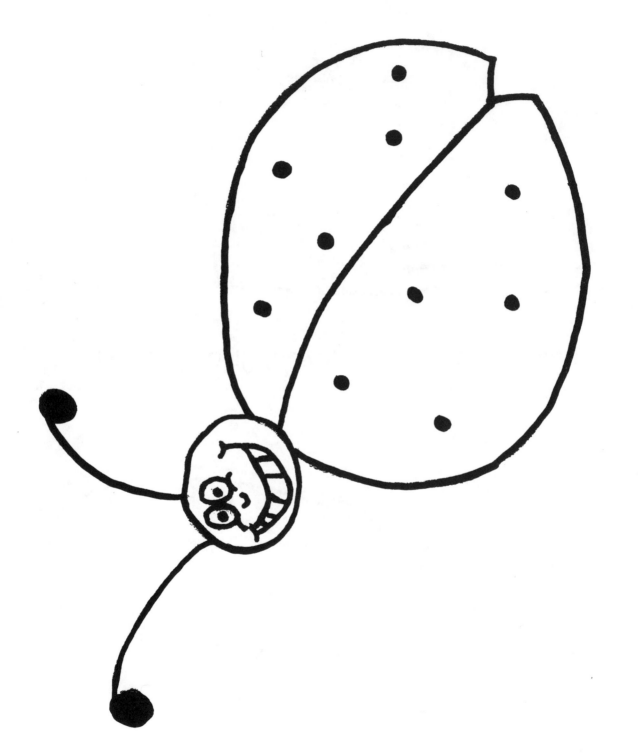

LINE MASTER—"THE SMUG BUG" BIG BOOK

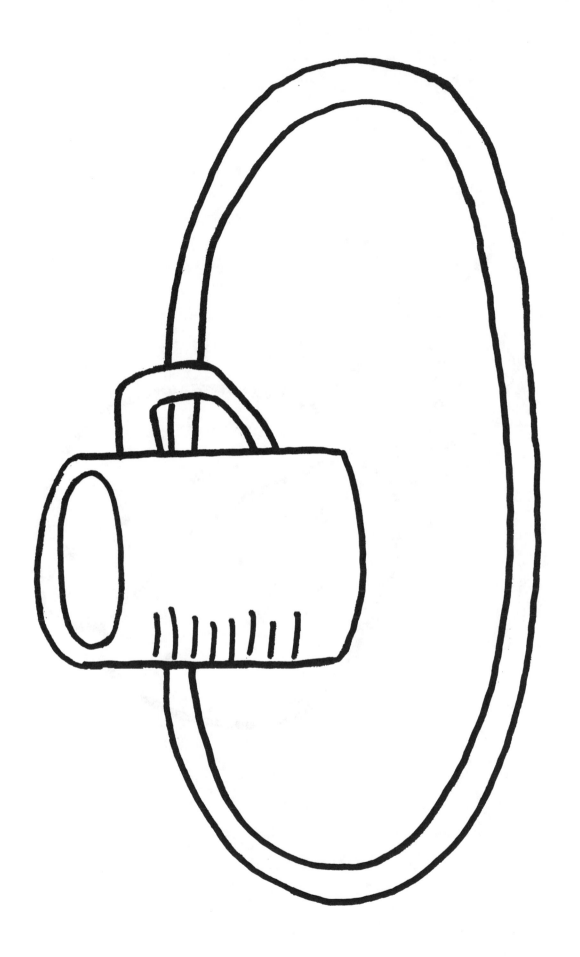

LINE MASTER—"THE SMUG BUG" BIG BOOK

LINE MASTER—"THE SMUG BUG" BIG BOOK

LINE MASTER—"THE SMUG BUG" BIG BOOK

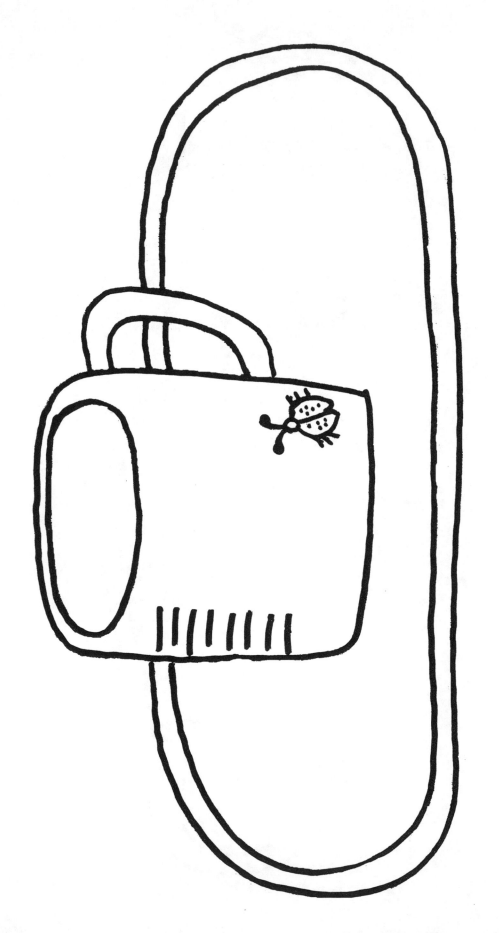

LINE MASTER—"THE SMUG BUG" BIG BOOK

LINE MASTER—"THE SMUG BUG" BIG BOOK

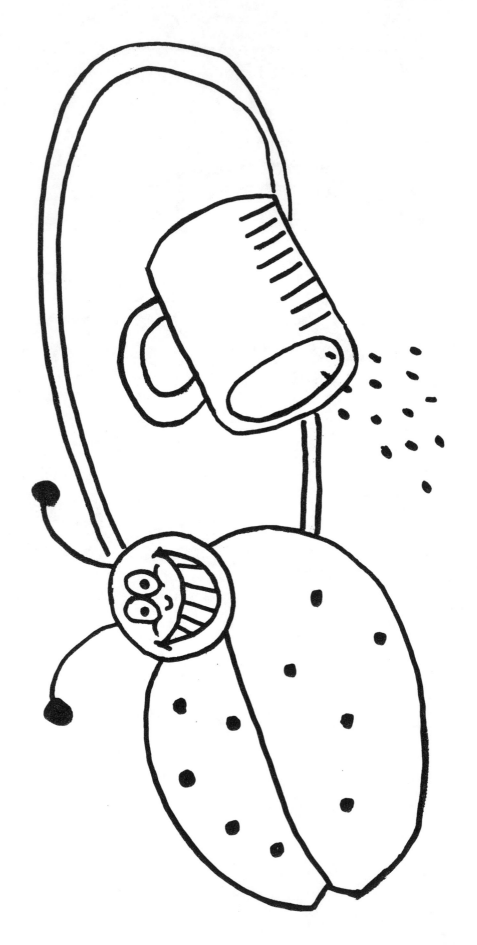

LINE MASTER—"THE SMUG BUG" BIG BOOK

Word Family
-ump

Lesson 1

Objectives
- To provide exposure and an introduction to the *-ump* word family
- To introduce the anchor word *jump*

Materials
- Chart-sized poem "Jump Rope"
- Chart paper
- Water-based marker

Procedure

1. Get a jump rope from the physical education teacher. Show the jump rope to the children. Ask the children if they have ever jumped rope. Have the children recite some of the playground rhymes they say while jumping rope. Have some of the children demonstrate.

2. Tell the children you will now read a poem titled "Jump Rope." Read "Jump Rope" to the children. Model 1:1 by pointing to each word as you read. Invite the children to read through the poem with you the second time.

> **Jump Rope**
>
> We play jump rope every day.
> This is the rhyme that **we** say.
> "Jump! Jump!
> Jump so high.
> Jump until you touch the sky!
> Jump! Jump!
> Turn around.
> Turn and then you touch the ground!"

3. Vary this activity by echo reading ("My turn, your turn") and choral reading.

4. Ask the children if they can find the word *jump* in the poem. Invite children to come up and circle the word *jump* with a water-based marker.

5. Now do the art activity with the children, either as a small group or whole class.

Art Activity

Materials

- Multicolor chenille stems or pipe cleaners (1 per child)
- Line master of poem "Jump Rope"
- Line master of children
- 12" × 18" yellow construction paper
- Stapler
- Crayons
- Masking tape

Preparation

Reproduce the poem "Jump Rope." Hold the yellow construction paper vertically and staple the poem to the top of the yellow construction paper.

Procedure

1. Children color in the children.
2. Put the ends of the chenille stem or pipe cleaner through the line master into the hands.
3. Tape the ends of the chenille stem or pipe cleaner on the back of the line master.
4. Send the poem and art activity home. This gives family members an opportunity to read the poem with the child.

Conclusion of Lesson

Bring children back to the large "Jump Rope" poem. Reread the poem together as a class.

Jump Rope

We play jump rope every day.
This is the rhyme that **we** say.
"Jump! Jump!
Jump so high.
Jump until you touch the sky!
Jump! Jump!
Turn around.
Turn and then you touch the ground!"

Jump Rope

We play jump rope every day.
This is the rhyme that **we** say.
"Jump! Jump!
Jump so high.
Jump until you touch the sky!
Jump! Jump!
Turn around.
Turn and then you touch the ground!"

LINE MASTER—CHILDREN

Lesson 2

Objectives

- Child will recognize -ump words visually and auditorily.
- Child will read words that belong in the -ump word family.

Materials

- Large copy of poem "Clara the Camel"
- Teacher-made model of the -ump blending strip
- Water-based marker

Procedure

1. Show children the poem "Clara the Camel."

Clara the Camel

Clara the camel had only one hump.
Some thought it was just a bump.
Some thought it was just a stump.
Some thought it was just a lump.
"My hump's not a bump nor a stump nor a lump.
We all have humps, whether one or two.
That's what makes us special—
both me and you!"

---

2. Tell the children they are going to hear a poem about a camel named Clara who had only one hump.
3. Read the poem to the children.
4. Ask children what they notice about the poem.
5. Read the poem again. This time emphasize the rhyming words.
6. Remind the children that words that sound alike at the end are called rhyming words.
7. Read the poem again and have the children listen for the words that rhyme. Have the children give you a "thumbs up" (or some other "secret signal") when they hear a rhyming word.
8. Circle with the water-based marker each rhyming word as it is read.
9. Read all the circled words aloud.
10. Write the circled rhyming words from the poem in a column on a separate piece of chart paper.
11. Ask the children what they notice that is the same about the words. Anything different?

12. Show the children that the only difference in each -*ump* word is the beginning sound. The middle and ending sounds are the same.

13. Ask the children for other words in the -*ump* word family.

14. Show the children the -*ump* blending strip and jump rope. Say "ump" out loud. Tell the children you will now show them words that belong to the -*ump* word family.

15. Move the blending strip to create all the -*ump* word-family words. Say the words as you create them. Have the children repeat them after you. Repeat this activity several times.

16. Explain to the children they will make their own -*ump* blending strip.

-ump Blending Strip Activity

Materials

- Line master of jump rope
- Blending strip with letters: *b, h, d, j, p, sl, st, th, pl* (You may edit the letters on the strip.)
- Blank writing paper
- Line master of -*ump* word family flashcards
- Crayons
- Scissors

Procedure

1. Give children the line master of the jump rope, scissors, and crayons.

2. Children color in the jump rope.

3. Children cut out the jump rope.

4. Cut two 1-inch vertical slits to the left of the chunk printed on the blending strip. Be sure to leave a 1-inch space between the slits.

5. Slide the strip through the slits.

6. Children read all the -*ump* words to you by sliding the strip through the jump rope.

7. Vary the activity by having children read to a partner, you, or any other adult.

8. Children then write all the words on the writing paper provided.

9. Send the blending strip and flashcards home to reinforce the -*ump* word family.

Challenge Activity

Children will turn the writing paper over and use each of the *-ump* words in a sentence. They can also make up a silly poem of their own using some or all of the *-ump* words.

Reinforcement Activity

1. For a small group mini-lesson, put the magnetic letters **j u m p** on an overhead projector (or on the floor facing the children if you do not have an overhead).

2. Tell children they know the word *jump*.

3. Run your finger under the word *jump* and say *j-u-m-p*, stretching out the word as you say it. Again, slide your finger under the word *jump* and stretch it out. Have children say it with you this time.

4. Remove the "j" from the word and tell children this chunk of the word is *ump*.

5. Put a "b" in front of the *-ump* on the overhead. Again, slide your finger under the word, stretching out *b-u-m-p* as you say it. Repeat this procedure with the letters *d, h, p, sl, st, th, ch, pl*. Have the children practice making *-ump* family words individually or with a partner using the magnetic letters as you demonstrated on the overhead projector.

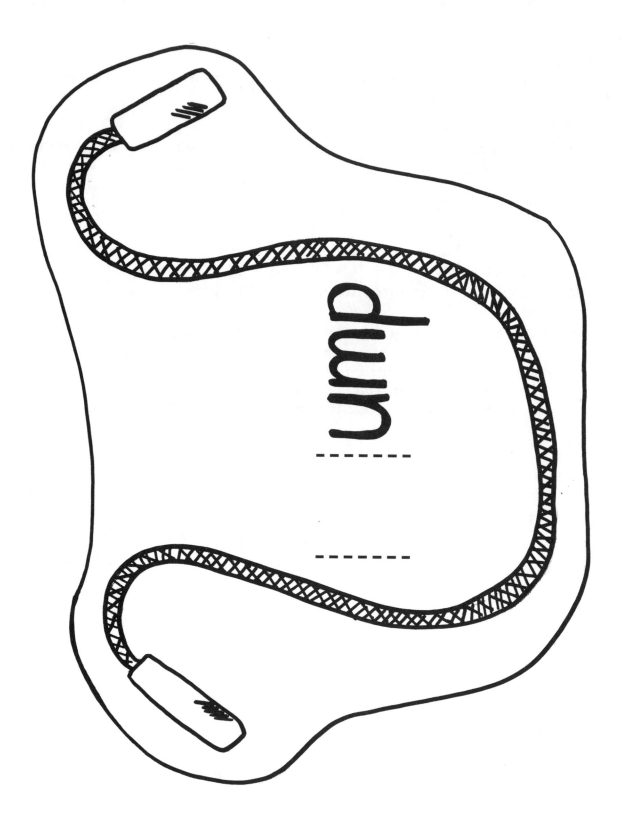

ump

- - - - - - -

- - - - - - -

LINE MASTER—JUMP ROPE BLENDING STRIP

bump	hump
dump	jump
pump	slump
stump	thump

LINE MASTER—*UMP* WORD FAMILY FLASHCARDS

Lesson 3

Objective

- Child will read -*ump* words in the context of a story.

Materials

- Big Book *Clara the Camel*
- Little Book *Clara the Camel*
- Crayons

Procedure

1. Introduce the Big Book *Clara the Camel*. Read the title to the children.

2. Remind the children they have been learning about the -*ump* word family. Elicit words from the -*ump* word family before you begin.

3. Take a picture walk through the book. Label all the pictures. Tell the children what is happening using some of the text from the book.

4. Read the book to the children, modeling 1:1, directionality, and return sweep.

5. Reread the book, inviting the children to read along with you. Do this several times. Vary the activity by echo reading or choral reading.

6. Give the children their own copy of the book. Have them read the book to themselves and then color in all the pictures. Have them read the book to a partner.

7. Listen to the children read the book independently or send the books home as a "read together," depending on the reading ability of each child.

Clara the Camel

Name _____

- -

Clara the camel had only one hump.

Some thought it was just a bump.

Some thought it was just a stump.

Some thought it was just a lump.

"My hump's not a bump nor a stump nor a lump."

LINE MASTER—"CLARA THE CAMEL" LITTLE BOOK

"We all have humps, whether one or two."

"That's what makes us special—both me and you!"

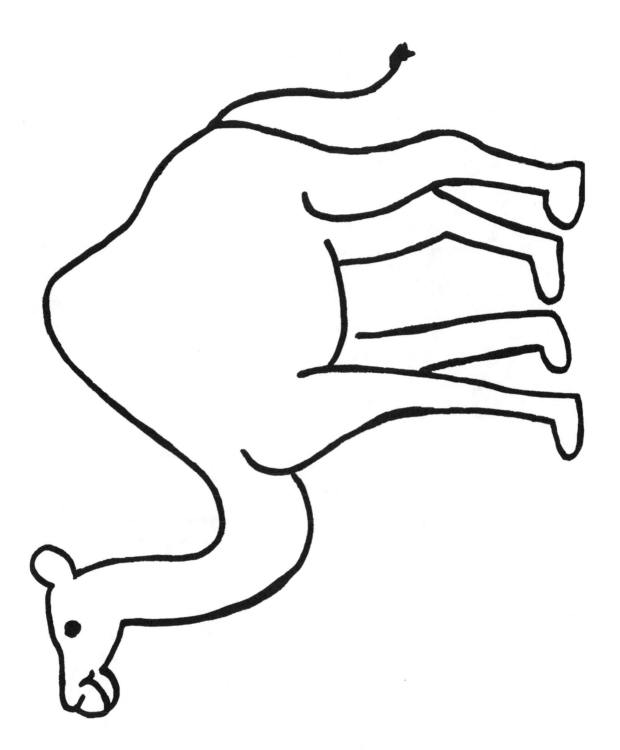

LINE MASTER—"CLARA THE CAMEL" BIG BOOK

LINE MASTER—"CLARA THE CAMEL" BIG BOOK

LINE MASTER—"CLARA THE CAMEL" BIG BOOK

LINE MASTER—"CLARA THE CAMEL" BIG BOOK

LINE MASTER—"CLARA THE CAMEL" BIG BOOK

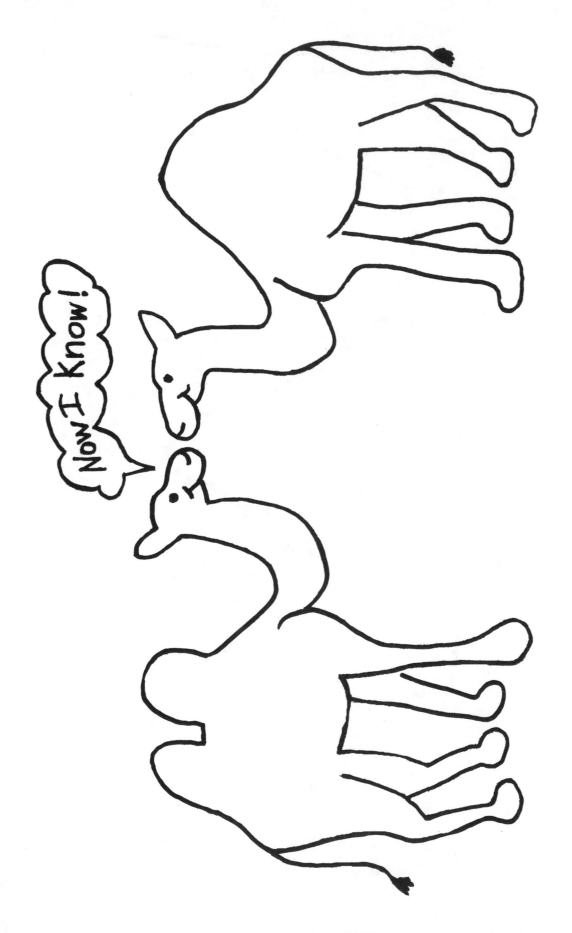

LINE MASTER—"CLARA THE CAMEL" BIG BOOK

LINE MASTER—"CLARA THE CAMEL" BIG BOOK

Word Family

-un

Lesson 1

Objectives

- To provide exposure and an introduction to the *-un* word family
- To introduce the anchor word *run*

Materials

- Chart-sized poem "The Race"
- Chart paper
- Water-based marker

Procedure

1. Read and discuss "The Tortoise and the Hare" by Aesop. Ask the children to share their racing experiences. These experiences can include playground races, physical education races, swimming races, etc.

2. Tell the children you will now read a poem titled "The Race." Read "The Race" to the children. Model 1:1 by pointing to each word as you read. Invite the children to read through the poem with you the second time.

The Race

Let's have a race!
It's lots of fun
to see who is the fastest one.
We can run in the sand.
No! It's too hot.
We can run in the mud . . .
or maybe not.
We can run in the water.
No! It's too wet.
Let's just run for fun.
On your mark, get set!

---

3. Vary this activity by echo reading ("My turn, your turn") and choral reading.

4. Ask the children if they can find the word *run* in the poem. Invite children to come up and circle the word *run* with a water-based marker.

5. Now do the art activity with the children, either as a small group or whole class.

Art Activity

Materials

- Line master of poem "The Race"
- Line master of sneaker
- 12" × 18" red construction paper
- Stapler
- 24-inch pieces of yarn (1 per child)
- Crayons
- Hole punch

Preparation

Reproduce the poem "The Race." Hold the red construction paper vertically and staple the poem to the top of the red construction paper.

Procedure

1. Children color in the sneaker.
2. Children cut out the sneaker.
3. Children punch holes on the dots provided.
4. Children lace the sneaker using the yarn.
5. Staple the sneaker onto the red paper.
6. Send the poem and art activity home. This gives family members an opportunity to read the poem with the child.

Conclusion of Lesson

Bring children back to the large "The Race" poem. Reread the poem together as a class.

The Race

Let's have a race!
It's lots of fun
to see who is the fastest one.
We can run in the sand.
No! It's too hot.
We can run in the mud . . .
or maybe not.
We can run in the water.
No! It's too wet.
Let's just run for fun.
On your mark, get set!

The Race

Let's have a race!
It's lots of fun
to see who is the fastest one.
We can run in the sand.
No! It's too hot.
We can run in the mud . . .
or maybe not.
We can run in the water.
No! It's too wet.
Let's just run for fun.
On your mark, get set!

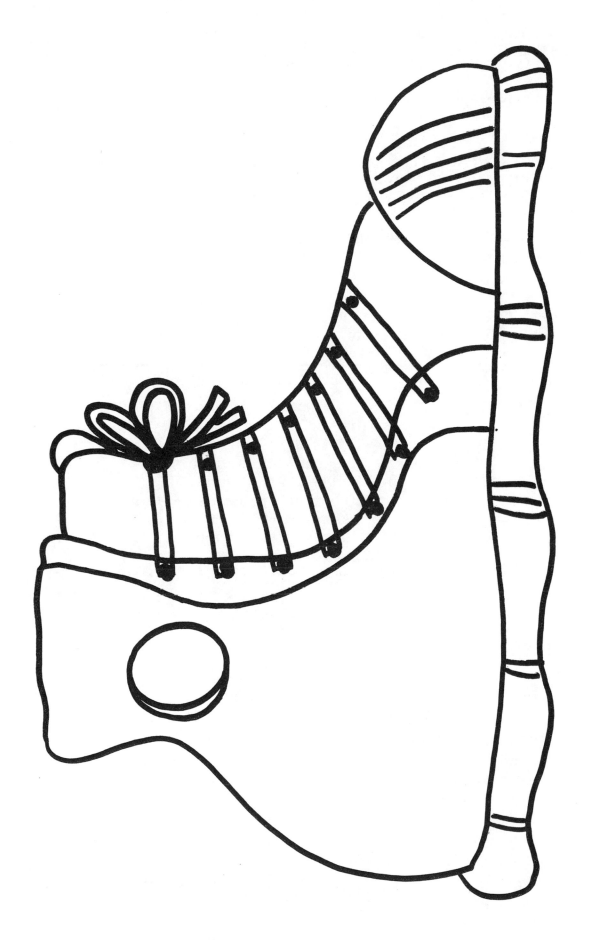

LINE MASTER—SNEAKER

Lesson 2

Objectives

- Child will recognize *-un* words visually and auditorily.
- Child will read words that belong in the *-un* word family.

Materials

- Large copy of poem "Spinning a Web"
- Teacher-made model of the *-un* blending strip
- Water-based marker

Procedure

1. Show children the poem "Spinning a Web."

Spinning a Web

There once was a spider
who thought it would be fun
to spin her web in the midday sun.
All day long she spun and spun.
"I'm tired and hot in the midday sun.
I'm beginning to think this isn't such fun!
Oh, no! I'm stuck in my web and I can't run!
This isn't what I had in mind
when I had begun!"

---

2. Tell the children they are going to hear a poem about a spider who spins a web.
3. Read the poem to the children.
4. Ask children what they notice about the poem.
5. Read the poem again. This time emphasize the rhyming words.
6. Remind the children that words that sound alike at the end are called rhyming words.
7. Read the poem again and have the children listen for the words that rhyme. Have the children give you a "thumbs up" (or some other "secret signal") when they hear a rhyming word.
8. Circle with the water-based marker each rhyming word as it is read.
9. Read all the circled words aloud.
10. Write the circled rhyming words from the poem in a column on a separate piece of chart paper.

11. Ask the children what they notice that is the same about the words. Anything different?

12. Show the children that the only difference in each -un word is the beginning sound. The middle and ending sounds are the same.

13. Ask the children for other words in the -un word family.

14. Show the children the -un blending strip and sun. Say "un" out loud. Tell the children you will now show them words that belong to the -un word family.

15. Move the blending strip to create all the -un word-family words. Say the words as you create them. Have the children repeat them after you. Repeat this activity several times.

16. Explain to the children they will make their own -un blending strip.

-un Blending Strip Activity

Materials

- Line master of sun
- Blending strip with letters: *b, g, p, r, s, f, st, sp* (You may edit the letters on the strip.)
- Blank writing paper
- Line master of -un word family flashcards
- Crayons
- Scissors

Procedure

1. Give children the line master of the sun, scissors, and crayons.

2. Children color in the sun.

3. Children cut out the sun.

4. Cut two 1-inch vertical slits to the left of the chunk printed on the blending strip. Be sure to leave a 1-inch space between the slits.

5. Slide the strip through the slits.

6. Children read all the -un words to you by sliding the strip through the sun.

7. Vary the activity by having children read to a partner, you, or any other adult.

8. Children then write all the words on the writing paper provided.

9. Send the blending strip and flashcards home to reinforce the -un word family.

Challenge Activity

Children will turn the writing paper over and use each of the -un words in a sentence. They can also make up a silly poem of their own using some or all of the -un words.

Reinforcement Activity

1. For a small group mini-lesson, put the magnetic letters **r u n** on an overhead projector (or on the floor facing the children if you do not have an overhead).

2. Tell children they know the word *run*.

3. Run your finger under the word *run* and say r-u-n, stretching out the word as you say it. Again, slide your finger under the word *run* and stretch it out. Have children say it with you this time.

4. Remove the "r" from the word and tell children this chunk of the word is *un*.

5. Put an "s" in front of the -un on the overhead. Again, slide your finger under the word, stretching out *s-u-n* as you say it. Repeat this procedure with the letters *b, g, p, f, st, sp*. Have the children practice making -un family words individually or with a partner using the magnetic letters as you demonstrated on the overhead projector.

LINE MASTER—SUN BLENDING STRIP

bun	fun
pun	run
sun	shun
stun	spun

LINE MASTER—*UN* WORD FAMILY FLASHCARDS

Lesson 3

Objective

- Child will read *-un* words in the context of a story.

Materials

- Big Book *Spinning a Web*
- Little Book *Spinning a Web*
- Crayons

Procedure

1. Introduce the Big Book *Spinning a Web*. Read the title to the children.

2. Remind the children they have been learning about the *-un* word family. Elicit words from the *-un* word family before you begin.

3. Take a picture walk through the book. Label all the pictures. Tell the children what is happening using some of the text from the book.

4. Read the book to the children, modeling 1:1, directionality, and return sweep.

5. Reread the book, inviting the children to read along with you. Do this several times. Vary the activity by echo reading or choral reading.

6. Give the children their own copy of the book. Have them read the book to themselves and then color in all the pictures. Have them read the book to a partner.

7. Listen to the children read the book independently or send the books home as a "read together," depending on the reading ability of each child.

Spinning a Web

Name _____

- -

There once was a spider who thought
it would be fun . . .

to spin her web in the midday sun.

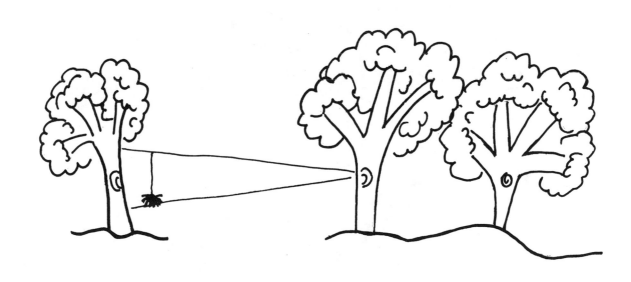

All day long she spun and spun.

"I'm tired and hot in the midday sun."

"I'm beginning to think this isn't such fun!"

"Oh, no! I'm stuck in my web and I can't run!"

"This isn't what I had in mind when I had begun!"

LINE MASTER—"SPINNING A WEB" LITTLE BOOK

LINE MASTER—"SPINNING A WEB" BIG BOOK

LINE MASTER—"SPINNING A WEB" BIG BOOK

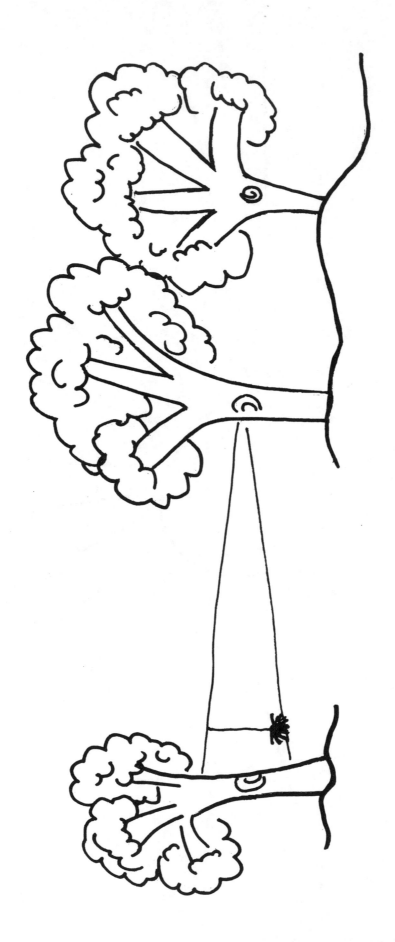

LINE MASTER—"SPINNING A WEB" BIG BOOK

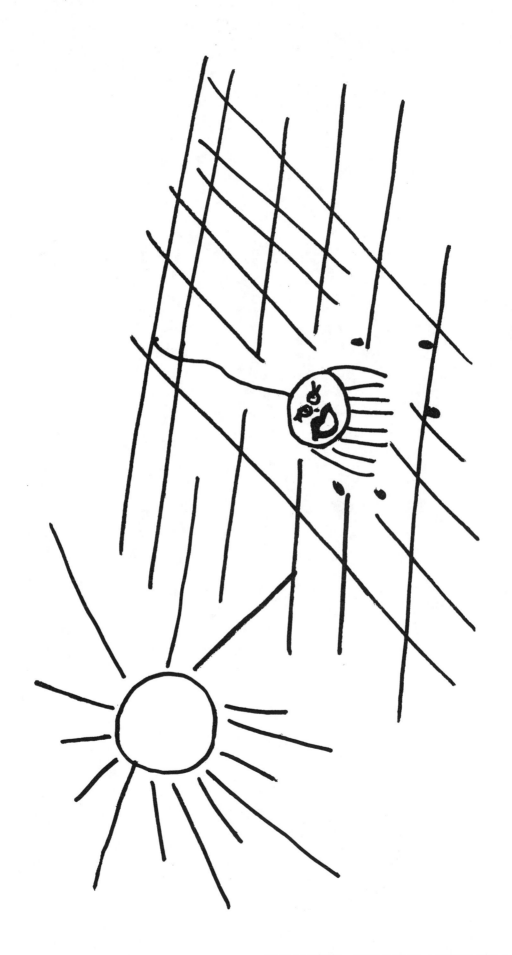

LINE MASTER—"SPINNING A WEB" BIG BOOK

LINE MASTER—"SPINNING A WEB" BIG BOOK

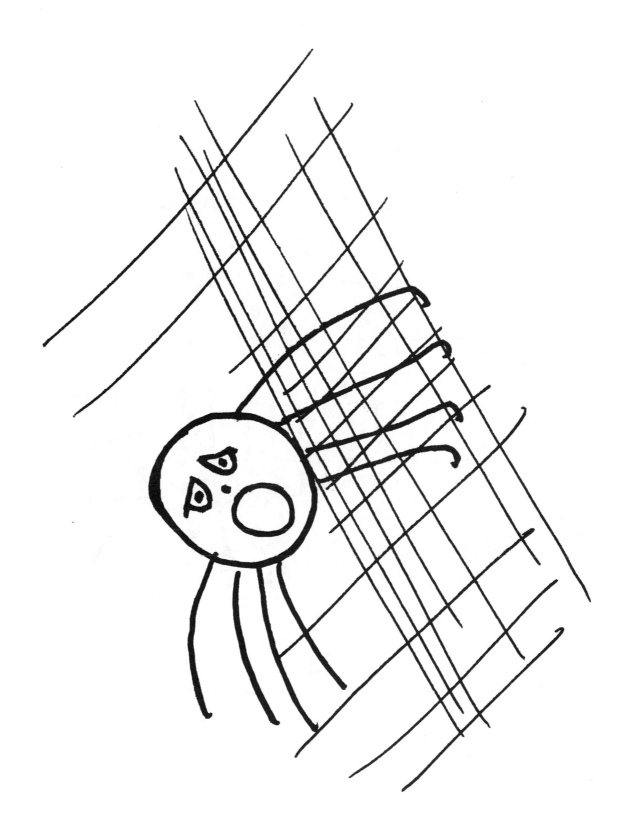

LINE MASTER—"SPINNING A WEB" BIG BOOK

-unk

Lesson 1

Objectives

- To provide exposure and an introduction to the *-unk* word family
- To introduce the anchor word *skunk*

Materials

- Chart-sized poem "Little Skunk"
- Chart paper
- Water-based marker

Procedure

1. Read and discuss a nonfiction book about skunks. Brainstorm facts about skunks. This will activate prior knowledge and fill in gaps for children. Use a graphic organizer, such as the web shown here.

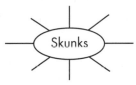

2. Tell the children you will now read a poem titled "Little Skunk." Read "Little Skunk" to the children. Model 1:1 by pointing to each word as you read. Invite the children to read through the poem with you the second time.

Little Skunk

He's little and furry
with a stripe down his back.
His stripe is white,
the rest is black.
When you see him coming,
get out of the way!
If you don't, he may spray!
Who is that animal all black and white
who ventures out when it is night?
It's a skunk, as you can tell.
He leaves behind his skunky smell.

3. Vary this activity by echo reading ("My turn, your turn") and choral reading.

4. Ask the children if they can find the word *skunk* in the poem. Invite children to come up and circle the word *skunk* with a water-based marker.

5. Now do the art activity with the children, either as a small group or whole class.

Art Activity

Materials

- White cotton balls
- Line master of poem "Little Skunk"
- Line master of skunk
- 12" × 18" red construction paper
- Stapler
- Black crayons
- Glue

Preparation

Reproduce the poem "Little Skunk." Hold the red construction paper vertically and staple the poem to the top of the red construction paper.

Procedure

1. Children color in the skunk.

2. Children glue the white cotton balls along the skunk's back and on his tail.

3. Let dry.

4. Staple the skunk onto the red paper.

5. Send the poem and art activity home. This gives family members an opportunity to read the poem with the child.

Conclusion of Lesson

Bring children back to the large "Little Skunk" poem. Reread the poem together as a class.

Little Skunk

He's little and furry
with a stripe down his back.
His stripe is white,
the rest is black.
When you see him coming,
get out of the way!
If you don't, he may spray!
Who is that animal all black and white
who ventures out when it is night?
It's a skunk, as you can tell.
He leaves behind his skunky smell.

Little Skunk

He's little and furry
with a stripe down his back.
His stripe is white,
the rest is black.
When you see him coming,
get out of the way!
If you don't, he may spray!
Who is that animal all black and white
who ventures out when it is night?
It's a skunk, as you can tell.
He leaves behind his skunky smell.

LINE MASTER—SKUNK

Lesson 2

Objectives

- Child will recognize -unk words visually and auditorily.
- Child will read words that belong in the -unk word family.

Materials

- Large copy of poem "Slam Dunk!"
- Teacher-made model of the -unk blending strip
- Water-based marker

Procedure

1. Show children the poem "Slam Dunk!"

Slam Dunk!

People say I have a lot of spunk.
I dribble down the court and . . .
Whoosh! Slam dunk!
I twist and I turn—shoot again—KERPLUNK!
I've sunk another. It landed with a clunk!
Clunk! Whoosh! Kerplunk! Slam dunk!
My team has won, thanks to my spunk.

---

2. Tell the children they are going to hear a poem about a child who plays basketball.
3. Read the poem to the children.
4. Ask children what they notice about the poem.
5. Read the poem again. This time emphasize the rhyming words.
6. Remind the children that words that sound alike at the end are called rhyming words.
7. Read the poem again and have the children listen for the words that rhyme. Have the children give you a "thumbs up" (or some other "secret signal") when they hear a rhyming word.
8. Circle with the water-based marker each rhyming word as it is read.
9. Read all the circled words aloud.
10. Write the circled rhyming words from the poem in a column on a separate piece of chart paper.

11. Ask the children what they notice that is the same about the words. Anything different?

12. Show the children that the only difference in each -unk word is the beginning sound. The middle and ending sounds are the same.

13. Ask the children for other words in the -unk word family.

14. Show the children the -unk blending strip and skunk. Say "unk" out loud. Tell the children you will now show them words that belong to the -unk word family.

15. Move the blending strip to create all the -unk word-family words. Say the words as you create them. Have the children repeat them after you. Repeat this activity several times.

16. Explain to the children they will make their own -unk blending strip.

-unk Blending Strip Activity

Materials

- Line master of skunk
- Blending strip with letters: b, h, d, j, s, cl, sp, sk, tr (You may edit the letters on the strip.)
- Blank writing paper
- Line master of -unk word family flashcards
- Crayons
- Scissors

Procedure

1. Give children the line master of the skunk, scissors, and crayons.

2. Children color in the skunk.

3. Children cut out the skunk.

4. Cut two 1-inch slits to the left of the chunk printed on the blending strip. Be sure to leave a 1-inch space between the slits.

5. Slide the strip through the slits.

6. Children read all the -unk words to you by sliding the strip through the skunk.

7. Vary the activity by having children read to a partner, you, or any other adult.

8. Children then write all the words on the writing paper provided.

9. Send the blending strip and flashcards home to reinforce the -unk word family.

Challenge Activity

Children will turn the writing paper over and use each of the -*unk* words in a sentence. They can also make up a silly poem of their own using some or all of the -*unk* words.

Reinforcement Activity

1. For a small group mini-lesson, put the magnetic letters **d u n k** on an overhead projector (or on the floor facing the children if you do not have an overhead).

2. Tell children they know the word *dunk*.

3. Run your finger under the word *dunk* and say *d-u-n-k*, stretching out the word as you say it. Again, slide your finger under the word *dunk* and stretch it out. Have children say it with you this time.

4. Remove the "d" from the word and tell children this chunk of the word is *unk*.

5. Put a "j" in front of the -*unk* on the overhead. Again, slide your finger under the word, stretching out *j-u-n-k* as you say it. Repeat this procedure with the letters *b, s, h, cl, sp, sk, tr*. Have the children practice making -*unk* family words individually or with a partner using the magnetic letters as you demonstrated on the overhead projector.

unk

LINE MASTER—SKUNK BLENDING STRIP

bunk	hunk
dunk	junk
sunk	clunk
spunk	skunk

Lesson 3

Objective

- Child will read -*unk* words in the context of a story.

Materials

- Big Book *Slam Dunk!*
- Little Book *Slam Dunk!*
- Crayons

Procedure

1. Introduce the Big Book *Slam Dunk!* Read the title to the children.

2. Remind the children they have been learning about the -*unk* word family. Elicit words from the -*unk* word family before you begin.

3. Take a picture walk through the book. Label all the pictures. Tell the children what is happening using some of the text from the book.

4. Read the book to the children, modeling 1:1, directionality, and return sweep.

5. Reread the book, inviting the children to read along with you. Do this several times. Vary the activity by echo reading or choral reading.

6. Give the children their own copy of the book. Have them read the book to themselves and then color in all the pictures. Have them read the book to a partner.

7. Listen to the children read the book independently or send the books home as a "read together," depending on the reading ability of each child.

Slam Dunk!

Name _____

People say I have a lot of spunk.

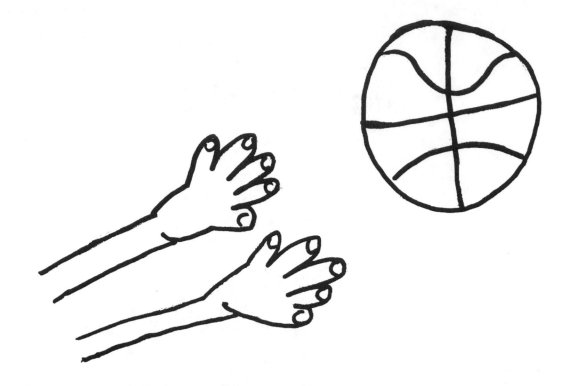

I dribble down the court and . . .

- -

Whoosh! Slam dunk!

I twist and I turn—shoot again—KERPLUNK!

I've sunk another. It landed with a clunk!

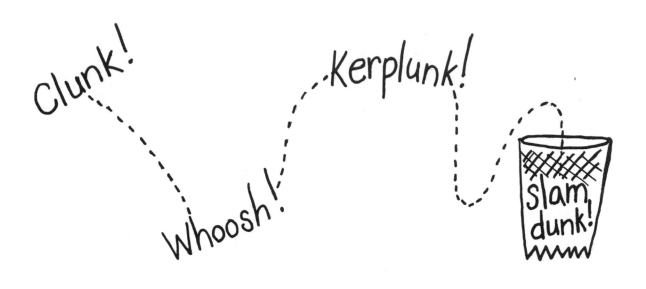

Clunk! Whoosh! Kerplunk! Slam dunk!

My team has won, thanks to my spunk.

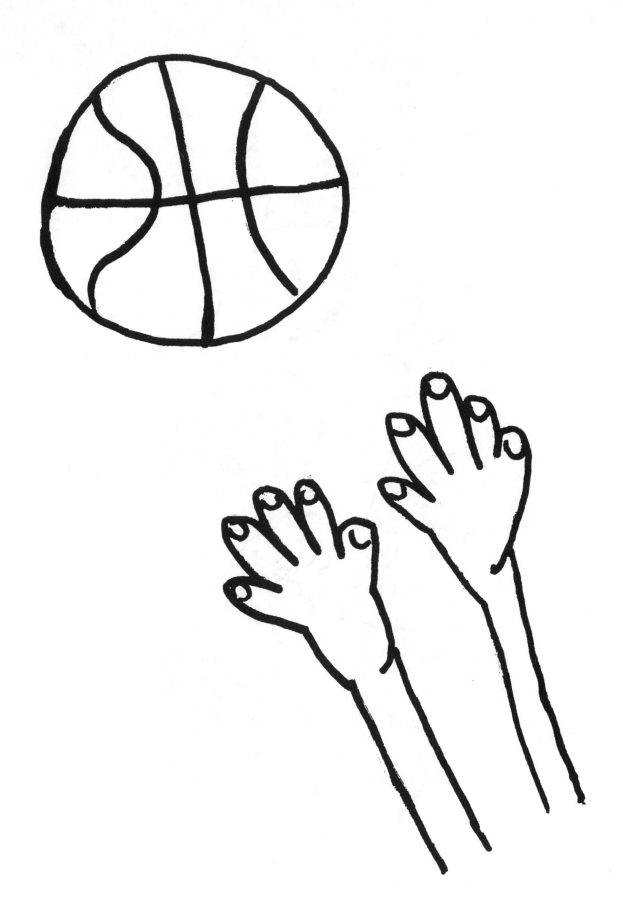

LINE MASTER—"SLAM DUNK!" BIG BOOK

LINE MASTER—"SLAM DUNK!" BIG BOOK

LINE MASTER—"SLAM DUNK!" BIG BOOK

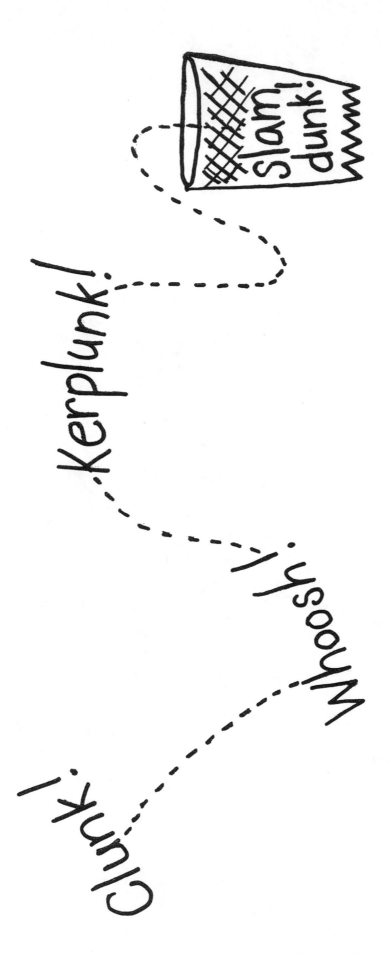

Slam dunk!

Kerplunk!

Whoosh!

Clunk!

LINE MASTER—"SLAM DUNK!" BIG BOOK